THE SAN JOAQUIN SIREN

AN

AMERICAN ACE
IN WWII'S CBI

To Dr. Murata
It has kept me waiting".
Thank you
Capt. Bill Behrns

BY
WILLIAM M. BEHRNS
WITH
KENNETH MOORE

An Amethyst Moon Book

AMETHYST MOON
PUBLISHING

THE SAN JOAQUIN SIREN

AN
AMERICAN ACE
IN WWII'S CBI

BY
WILLIAM M. BEHRNS
WITH
KENNETH MOORE

An Amethyst Moon Book
Published by AMETHYST MOON PUBLISHING
P.O. Box 87885
Tucson, AZ 85754
www.ampubbooks.com

ISBN 978-1-935354-61-1 (13 digit)
1-935354-61-2 (10 digit)

Library of Congress Control Number: 2011937414

This book is dedicated to Kenneth S. Moore

The San Joaquin Siren would not have become a reality if Ken had not persisted for more than three years to urge Bill to tell his story. Unfortunately Ken passed away unexpectedly when, as he put it, the book was "four-fifths done." I, his wife, worked with Bill to finish the book, which in reality was more than four-fifths done. Ken had a master's degree in history and especially loved the P-38, likely because of his early introduction to the plane in his hometown of Santa Maria, California. Ken was told that the book was going to be published the day before he died. One of his life long dreams was to be a published author. This he accomplished.

-- Tina Moore

Contents

Author's Note

I possess all of the records of my military service, which substantiate the claims made in this book. Events were chronicled and brought to life by the writing of my very good friend and fellow author, Ken Moore.

-- *William M. Behrns*

Lieutenant William M. Behrns (Bill Behrns' collection)

Prologue

World War II began at different times and in different places depending upon who was involved. For the Japanese and Chinese it began in 1936 in Manchuria. In Western Europe, it began more slowly, with German movements into the Sudeten lands and Czechoslovakia in 1939, preceding the 1940 attacks on Poland and France, and finally England. For the United States of America, the conflict began with the Japanese attack on Pearl Harbor, December 7, 1941.

By the time it was finally over, hundreds of millions of people had been involved in the conflict in some way. Casualty estimates ran up to one hundred million, depending on where the information was obtained. The important thing to remember about the war is that it changed the entire world and everyone who was caught up in it. For those who fought, particularly in frontline combat units, it was a transformational experience like no other. No one so involved escaped the stress and trauma without damage, scars, and emotional distresses that would remain for the rest of their lives. Many veterans closed themselves off from painful war memories, refusing to talk to anyone about the horrors they saw and experienced. It remained too real and too painful to revisit. Others waited a full 50 years to finally speak out and publicly remember. Even today some are still silent.

There are many veterans' groups active in the world today, encompassing all branches of the armed services in each and every country. Veterans regularly gather together to share memories and provide information about places served and friends remembered. It is an act of brotherhood as well as an act of faith to those who served, whether in WWII, Korea, Vietnam, Desert Storm, Iraq, Afghanistan, or many other conflicts fought by and for others. It is a necessary exercise that must be carried out, particularly for the WWII generation. The great armies that fought so long and so well are diminishing in size at a rapid rate. In America, more than 1500 a week are marching into history. As more stories are being told, even more are being forever lost. Personal histories, the most precious of records, die with the participants unless dutifully related and recorded. Herodotus said that history was written so "the great deeds of the Greeks and the Barbarians should not be forgotten." It is for this reason the following memoir is presented to the world.

Introduction

Since I first saw a P-38 Lightning in flight at a 1948 air show in my hometown of Santa Maria, California, I have had an abiding interest in the Lockheed Lightning. My father took me to the old Allan Hancock Flying Field on Bradley Road to see airplanes up close and watch them fly. He drove the old 1936 Plymouth we owned down to the field, which was situated on the northeast corner of town on property that is now the campus of Allan Hancock College, where I would attend classes 12 years later. Little did I know the influence that day would have on the rest of my life.

Sixty-three years later, I don't remember much about that day beyond what I saw of the bright red P-38 that appeared there that morning. I first noticed the aircraft when I looked down the east to west asphalt landing strip toward the distant but visible Coast Range and saw what appeared to be a thin line in the air. It was clearly moving, definitely an airplane. A closer looked revealed two bumps, one on either side, halfway out on the line. A larger, more definite bulge appeared in the center of what, a few seconds later, proved to be two engines. This was the plane's cockpit gondola in which the pilot rode. Fascinated, I watched the surreal craft approach and soon heard the deep, powerful hum of twin Allison engines, a sound I was never to forget.

The red plane with the yellow lightning bolt painted on the nose roared past us at high speed, perhaps 50 feet above the ground. Just as it passed, the pilot suddenly pulled up into a forty-five degree climb and banked his craft sharply to the left, revealing a visually unique configuration. It was a beautiful and impressive sight for the five year old that I then was. I can see it in my mind's eye yet.

"What's that?" I asked Dad, nearly shouting.

"That's a P-38 Lightning," he answered. "It goes five hundred miles an hour!" I didn't really know then just how fast five hundred miles an hour really was, but it seemed like a very high speed when compared to the seventy-five miles per hour I had once experienced riding in our old Plymouth. Right then and there I decided I wanted to fly, and I wanted to fly that plane. That was not to be. I never did become a pilot, and it would be fifty-six years before I saw another Lightning take to the air. Through all of that, my interest in the Lightning remained. I would eventually begin a novel about P-38s in the Pacific Theater and join four different 'warbird' groups in search of further information.

One day in early 2003, I was standing on a walkway at the Sacramento Trapshooting Club with my old friend Glen Vanderford, whom I had met when I first took up competitive shooting. We were passing time between squads by watching a very well-restored Grumman Wildcat practicing landings at nearby McClellan Air Force Base. As we watched Glen told me he had landed many times on that very same field during WWII. "Its an easy field to land on," Glen told me. "I used to grease that old P-38 right in there."

I had suddenly found a Lightning driver. A little later he told me there was a local P-38 group and invited me to have breakfast with them on Thursday. I accepted and the story moved onward.

Glen's breakfast group was called the P-38/F-5 Fork Tail Devils, an organization based in Rancho Cordova, California, and devoted to the maintenance and enhancement of the P-38 legacy. The group consisted of former Lightning drivers and their friends and associates who shared a common interest in the legendary plane that was the most versatile and effective aircraft in World War II. It was at that morning meeting that I first met Captain Bill Behrns. When I heard his story that day I was hooked. I had to follow up.

Bill Behrns served in the China Burma India (CBI) region of the Pacific war. The southern part of CBI was a backwater of the conflict encompassing most of Burma, French Indo-China (Vietnam), Cambodia, and Assam. Into this remote area the US Army Air Corps sent thirty-two pilots in twenty-five Lightnings as the newly formed 459th Squadron, 80th Fighter Group, to face five hundred fifty enemy aircraft known to be operating there. The men came from thirty-two different states, the only such unit in the war. That they were expendable was obvious since the loss of a single pilot would scarcely be noticed in any single state while the loss of several from one state would likely result in civil outcries and inquiries from Congress. It was a cynical, but necessary, strategy. Someone had to tie down those enemy aircraft and keep them from moving to nearby areas more critical to the Allied war effort. Thirty-two P-38 drivers did just that.

Naming his P-38 *San Joaquin Siren* in honor of his home county, Captain Behrns and his squadron mates took to the air, day after day, on bombing runs and strafing missions mixed in with constant dog fighting, shoot-downs, accidents, and painful losses. Outnumbered in theater seventeen-to-one, there was never a day when the Twin Dragons were top-heavy underdogs. Still, they soldiered on until Japan was defeated. At the end of the fighting, only four survived to return home. Even in that great conflict such courage and sacrifice was rare.

No less than Lord Louis Mountbatten, overall commander

of CBI, paid personal tribute to the courage of the pilots and crewmen of the 459nd Squadron by autographing a commemorative shade canopy signed by all squadron members and many superior officers under which they served. Not far from Lord Mountbatten's mark is the signature of "Vinegar Joe " Stillwell, the ranking American General in the CBI. That historical relic was, until recently, owned by the last surviving member of the original 32 pilots of the Twin Dragon Squadron, Captain Bill Behrns, who has transferred its ownership to a P-38 Museum in Lodi, California, owned and operated by Bill's great friend and ultimate P-38 historian, Cecil Kramer.

Bill's story is a saga of incredible courage, resourcefulness, and dedication to duty by Bill, himself, and all of those who served with him on the ground or in the air. At the age of 90, it is time for this air ace and American hero to tell his story. It's time to hitch a ride in the *San Joaquin Siren* and go to war with Bill.

Kenneth S. Moore
Stockton, California
January 16, 2011

BOOK ONE: Genesis

Chapter One: Beginning Life in California

The Good Book starts its story with the now classic words, *In the beginning*. The beginning for me was in the small hamlet of French Camp, California, on April 18, 1920. I was born to William J. and Ida Mae Behrns who owned a small dairy farm of about 15 acres. At this point, my life would have seemed to be much like all of those people born during that era, but I wasn't at all like everyone else. I was three months premature and my birth weight was almost three pounds. The doctor looked me over and then told my parents they would never be able to raise this baby.

My parents refused to believe that I was done before I started. They took me from the midwife's residence and carted me home in cardboard box originally made for work boots and took me inside of the home in which I would grow up. There my father started a fire in the old cast iron cook stove, opened the baking oven, and placed me in my box on the flat surface of the open door. He then lined the box with blankets my mother had brought to him and created a homemade 1920 incubator in which I spent my first several days.

Being less then fully developed internally, I could not tolerate the normal mother's milk I was first given. I threw up every time I tried to eat. Cow's milk fared no better, and soft food was even worse. Finally a nearby neighbor suggested we try milk from his goats, and there I found my diet for the next two years. Unfortunately, goat's milk lacked the necessary calcium and minerals needed for proper bone growth, and I soon developed a serious case of rickets which left me badly underweight and fragile. My parents continued to worry about me.

To everyone's surprise, I turned out to be a very active child, perhaps the most active one around. I ran everywhere I went and played every game I could find my way into. My lack of size did not inhibit my childhood activities in the slightest. I had no serious injuries, and no broken bones. I also escaped all of the normal

Bill at six months (Bill Behrns' collection)

childhood diseases. I didn't have one of them. All these years later I still thank those goats for the unusual health that was to be mine. It is said that in every litter there is a runt and I believe I was qualified for that title.

By the time I was 14 and ready for high school, I weighed fifty-five pounds, less than half the weight of my smallest classmates. I was even smaller than the girls. The rickets had left me, and I was beginning to gain some height. I would eventually reach nearly five feet ten. I also began to grow some serious hair that allowed me to look more normal. I was delighted that my Chihuahua days were over. Many times I had found myself in scuffles with kids who razzed me about my nearly bald head. Fortunately, in spite of my small size, I could and did whip most of them. Still, it was nice to be past that problem.

I spent four years at Stockton High School more or less

without incident. I was an average student who had little time for extracurricular activities, due to my farm chores, so that time passed with little excitement. I was able to acquire a driver's license at age 14 and each day I drove into Stockton, taking two other students with me. For doing that I was given a three-dollars-a-month transportation payment by the school to defray fuel costs. The two passengers who rode with me were also allowed the same fee and they gave their three dollars each to me, which gave me nine dollars a month to spend on gas and whatever else I might afford. The money was more than adequate, and I had money left to spend. In 1934, the deepest part of the Great Depression, I felt practically rich.

Actually, driving to and from school was one of my greatest pleasures while attending high school. I dearly loved to drive, and I enjoyed driving fast. I could squeeze 50 miles per hour out of the Model A sedan my parents provided for me, and I drove it maxed out at every opportunity. I would pick up my two or sometimes three passengers, turn onto El Dorado Street, and head southbound for French Camp with my foot flat on the floor and the Ford engine straining for more speed. This daily routine was certain to come to the attention of law enforcement sooner or later since the speed limit inside the city limits was thirty-five miles per hour. While I never encountered any difficulties getting to school in the morning, on occasion I would encounter a challenge on the way home. Two or three times a month the local police would sit on a side street and watch for speeders to whom they could issue traffic tickets. I came to be one of their prime targets since I was always flat out at 50 as I approached the edge of town where the cops lurked.

Back in those days the police were somewhat limited in

what they were allowed to do in order to put a collar on the likes of me. Hot pursuit was not allowed, and if a speeder reached the city line before being pulled over, the police had to give up the chase and allow the law-breaker to escape. I took full advantage of this rule and anytime the red light came on behind me, I stayed on the floorboards until I streaked across the city limit, ahead of the traffic cops. I thoroughly enjoyed these infrequent contests and during my four years defying street law, I never got a ticket.

The game eventually spread to my tiny hometown of French Camp, which consisted of a post office, a fire station, a small general store, a public school, and four or five houses. I went through there just as flat out as I had been leaving Stockton. After a while word of "that crazy Behrns kid blasting through town" spread to the local Highway Patrolman who took to hiding behind a large billboard just beyond Beattie's General Store in hopes of bagging Little Bill. Somehow I always knew when he was there. I do not know how I knew this, but I always did and crawled through town at twenty-five miles per hour waving to the black and white as I passed it. I never got a ticket there either.

I graduated from Stockton High in 1938, just after my eighteenth birthday. By then I had reached my adult height of five feet ten inches, and I weighed a bit over a hundred pounds. My health continued to be excellent.

I decided to continue my education and enrolled in the College of the Pacific in the Conservatory of Music, where I studied music history. I played piano and string base in a dance band owned by Herbert (Bud) Ross whom I would know for many years afterward. At regular intervals, while playing a dance job, Bud would want a smoke break. He would turn the piano over to me for the ten or so minuets he needed for a nicotine fix and, when he returned, I would resume simple cords on the base fiddle. There were ten to twelve of us in the band depending on the night and the gig. We had several fine musicians with us, and we played pretty good music. We were busy often and made good spending money playing.

From Pacific I moved to UC Davis, seeking to improve my agricultural background. I didn't really have a goal in those days but thought it likely I would follow in my family's footsteps and become a farmer. When the school year ended in May of 1940, I returned to the farm. I had studied dairy product manufacturing; production of cheese, butter and ice cream; refrigeration; agronomy; and sheep production. School ended early in May to allow students to work on the family farms during summer.

I reached home on Friday afternoon with no prospects for excitement. On Saturday morning all of that changed. Two good friends invited me to join them at an air show down in Modesto, and for lack of anything better to do I decided to attend. I had never been to an airport before and had never had any interest in whatever people did at such places, but this was something to do on a Sunday that was at least new and different. At that moment I had no idea that my life was about to change.

Chapter Two: Awakening

Sunday morning proved to be one of those lovely, late spring days residents of our San Joaquin Valley live for and learn to expect. It was bright, clear and warm. Visibility was unlimited, and comfort was guaranteed. Lifelong friends, Lester Rodgers and Ken Kruder, picked me up, and we drove to Modesto Airport to see the air show the guys had promised me.

We arrived at the field about 11:00 a.m., just in time to see the beginning of the show. The runway there was a one-way asphalt strip laid out, as I recall, southeast to northwest. Along either side of the strip was a mown grass border, perhaps 50 yards wide, providing a safety lane for run-offs as well as a run-up area for planes waiting to take off. Beyond that there were bleacher seats for perhaps a thousand people. The bleachers were full, and the crowd was noisy. We found seats high in the stands where we could see the entire field.

The play-by-play announcer was calling out pilots' names and plane types over several loudspeakers, and I soon found my attention directed to a Waco bi-plane that was warming up on the grass border across the field from our seats. At that point the announcer introduced two of the participants, the first of them being pilot Roscoe Turner. I had never heard of the man before that day, but I soon found out that Turner had a more-than-impressive resume. To his credit were wins in the Thompson and Bendix Cup air races, aerobatic displays of outstanding quality, and many stunt-flying episodes in Hollywood movies.

Turner proved to be a flamboyant performer from the

moment he first appeared. He taxied his pure white Ryan racing plane onto the runway, and I was immediately fascinated by the configuration of this low-wing, open-cockpit racing plane that fairly shouted to the crowd about speed and performance. The aircraft was painted pure white, and the pilot matched his plane perfectly. Turner was clad in a pure white flying suit topped by a pure white leather helmet beneath which was a pure white silk scarf, flowing in the light breeze. Turner was a true performer with all of the dash and flare of a Hollywood spectacular. One look at the man and we all knew we were in for a memorable show.

Roscoe Turner performed an entire suite of aerobatic maneuvers in every possible degree of difficulty. The longer he flew, the more difficult and dangerous his acrobatic flying became. Flying upside down, close to the ground, made the women in the audience scream and the men hold their breath. Tilting the plane on first one wing and then another, Turner completed inside and outside loops that barely cleared the ground. He ended his performance with low, high-speed passes just above sets of bleacher seats, causing his audience to fearfully wonder if he was about to crash directly into them. He ended each pass by going into a barrel roll and finally landed smoothly and stepped out of the plane. He then mounted into the jump seat of a pure white LaSalle convertible sedan and rode down the past the stands waving to the crowd. It was pure Hollywood the whole way.

During this performance, the Waco bi-plane continued to sit across the runway from us, still idling and waiting to be flown. At that moment a seemingly drunken cowboy emerged from the bleachers and began staggering toward the idling plane. He was carrying a big brown bottle in his right hand from which he took a jolt as he moved closer to the aircraft.

The audience began screaming and shouting in protest at the presence of this out-of-control individual. They wanted that drunk off the field. The announcer paid no attention to the protests and went on describing the wondrous performance just completed by the great Roscoe Turner. It was a scary moment for us as we watched potential disaster approach, but the announcer soon became aware of the problem and summoned a police officer to remove the offending drunkard. The cop hauled the cowboy off the field, and things came back to normal, or so we thought. The show seemed ready to resume.

As the announcer began describing the next act, the cowboy suddenly reappeared, and this time he made it around the tail of the plane and moved to the lower wing. He paused a moment to take another pull from the brown bottle which he then tossed on the ground before climbing onto the lower wing and turning to wave at the crowd while nearly falling to the ground. Amid the screams and shouts of the onlookers, he then climbed further onto the bi-plane and proceeded to attempt to climb into the plane. The man reached the handhold bar on the upper wing and swung one foot into the cockpit. Hanging on with one hand and holding his big cowboy hat in the other, he seemed again about to fall when the plane suddenly began to taxi down the runway. The cowboy began pounding on the upper wing with his hat and shouting, "Get me out of here! Get me out of here!" over and over. The plane then gained speed and took off with him still hanging out on the wing. He eventually managed to climb properly aboard and made a quick touchdown landing, at the far end of the field, to allow the hidden pilot to deplane before going back to the air and into his remarkable act.

The announcer then let us in on the gag, telling us that this flyer was Tex Rankin, America's premier comedy aerobatic flyer. Rankin kept us on the edge of our seats for nearly half an hour doing rolls, loops, and tumbles that seemed improbable if not impossible. He ended his hair-raising performance with a more difficult and dangerous move than any we had seen that day, from an inverted position, perhaps six feet above the runway, at high speed. At the end of the runway a tripod had been set up on top of which was a white flag sticking out at an angle slightly less than vertical. As he approached the flag, Tex tilted his wing and reached out and grabbed the flag as he roared past. He then put his aircraft into a reverse (or inside) Immelman, experiencing several "g's" of force that threatened to pull him right out of his plane. He then landed to thunderous and lasting applause.

Watching these two flyers perform completely mesmerized me to the extent that I loudly announced to everyone near enough to hear that I wanted to be a pilot and fly like those men had. From that moment on I had my first conscious goal in life. I would join the Army Air Corps and become a pilot.

The following morning I went to the Army recruiting office and signed up for the Air Corps. To finalize my enlistment it was necessary to take a physical examination that revealed that my 110-pound weight was too low for my 5-feet-10-inch height. I was turned down on the spot. I was deeply disappointed, but there was little to be done at that time. I moved on to the world of work.

Chapter Three: The Next Step

To further my education it would be necessary to obtain gainful employment, which I found with Standard Oil of Stockton, California. I was fortunate to be chosen as part of a sales team. I was so chosen because of my university credits and ability to talk easily with people. Throughout the Depression people had neglected their cars due to lack of money for repairs, and now that times were beginning to improve, it was my job to suggest proper improvements to customers as they pulled into our station for gas and oil. I would open the hoods of customers' cars and inspect for leaks, worn belts, cracked hoses, and the like. I was able to sell with consistency, and my monthly checks averaged $172.00 per month, several dollars above the minimum because of commissions I earned. That was pretty decent money for 1940.

At the end of August, it was time to return to school. I had recently discovered, to my surprise, that teachers made $140.00 per month and with a master's degree they pulled in $150.00. With all of the wisdom granted to a twenty year old, I decided it was pointless to return to school when I was already earning more than these "professionals." Instead, I went down to a local dealer and purchased a new Pontiac convertible and made ready to conquer the world.

After fifteen months with Standard Oil, I turned twenty-one years old and was eligible to take a civil service exam. I passed the test easily, and a short time later I received a letter telling me to report to the Benicia Arsenal as a federal employee. Upon arrival I was appointed a munitions warehouse manager at a salary of $240.00 a month. There were thirty-five people under my direction, all of whom were Negros, and all of whom had been on the job longer than I had been. They were wonderfully hard workers, and we got along splendidly. I must say that I developed a strong respect for the work ethic and the patriotism of my crew.

My first day on the job was enlightening. The superintendent of the Arsenal took me out to the plant and introduced me to my new department. We stood on one side of a large truck drive-through and the workers lined up on the other side with perhaps ten feet between us. The "Super" announced my appointment by saying, "Here's your new boss. From now on you will take all of your orders from him."

With that he turned and walked away, leaving me with a large group of people, the likes of which I had never seen in my life. The man hadn't even spoken my name. We stood staring at each other across the truck run. The heavy silence was oppressive and did nothing to calm my nerves. I hadn't the slightest idea of what to say or do, and right there things might have stood, had not one of the men stepped across toward me and introduced himself to me. He told me that he had been chosen by the crew as their unofficial foreman, and if I would work through him we could move forward in an orderly fashion. "If you talk to them," he said, "they will stand and stare." He then went on to explain the system. "If you want something done, you tell me, and I will tell them. Then things will work just fine."

During my stay at the arsenal, he always went wherever I went, and I always told him what I wanted the crew to do. I called him Shadow for he always seemed to be an extension of me. We had a fine working relationship, and the crew worked well as long as all things passed through him.

As time passed, the coolness toward me that I found in the crew continued. Each day at lunch Shadow and I sat on one side of the truck run and ate together while the crew sat on the opposite side to eat theirs. They seldom spoke with each other and never spoke to me, preferring to sit silently and stare across the entryway. I felt like an exhibit rather than a boss. No one was ever hostile or aggressive, but there was definitely a space between us.

Four days into this routine I started smoking, and that event led to a change between us. I was smoking Wings cigarettes that I could buy in the PX for nine cents a pack. I chose this brand because I was still intent on becoming a pilot, and I enjoyed the association of the name. Each lunch break, Shadow and I sat on our side of the driveway, and I shared a smoke with him, while the crew sat on their side and watched in silence. Shadow enjoyed his smoke immensely and always thanked me for including him. We were becoming friends, and I was enjoying his company.

After a couple of days, I became aware that the generalized stare of the crewmen had become focused on our cigarettes. I began to wonder if perhaps the men would enjoy a smoke of their own. With this in mind, the next morning I purchased an additional package of Wings and took them to the plant for the afternoon meal. As Shadow and I took ours, I announced in a loud voice, "Maybe the men would like a smoke." I addressed this to Shadow in the usual way, and I continued, saying to him "Here's an additional pack. See that each man has one."

Shadow complied, smiling, and every man smoked. The result of this was nearly immediate. On the next morning, when I arrived at the plant, each man waved a greeting as I passed and said, "Mornin,' Boss." This continued every day

I worked with the crew. It would be the only conversation I would ever have with them.

The job at the Arsenal lasted four months. I worked six days a week and had Sundays off. Sundays I spent at home in French Camp, and I was there when our world changed forever.

Chapter Four: Suddenly — War!

December 7th, 1941, found me at home in French Camp, totally unprepared for what I was then to hear. I was quietly listening to the family radio when a reporter broke into the broadcast telling us Pearl Harbor was under attack by the Japanese. Like nearly everyone I knew or have meant since, I can remember just about everything about that fateful morning. It was a landmark in the lives of all of us. We knew at that moment our lives were forever changed. We were suddenly involved in the spreading conflict that would soon be called World War II. In the midst of the broadcast, my father handed me an envelope from the previous day's mail that contained orders for me to report for duty with the U S Army. I was to meet a bus in Manteca for the ride to Fort Ord Army base near Monterey. I had about a week to prepare myself for the transition to military life.

The next morning I took the draft notice to the superintendent's office at the Benicia Arsenal and presented it to the foreman. He told me that I was already in essential government service and he would sign me off so that I could continue in my present job. I told him thanks a lot but no thanks. I viewed this as my next step toward achieving my goal of joining the Air Corps and becoming a pilot. If things worked out well I would be able to fly airplanes, and I was going into the service to make that happen.

My stay at Fort Ord was brief. I was sworn in, received shots, and was promptly transferred to Camp Callan near San Diego for basic training. Three weeks of calisthenics and drills ended thankfully for me when I was sent to a school that happened to be instruction in the care, maintenance, and operation of each vehicle in the motor pool. The class contained two hundred of us broken up into small units. Here I found something odd. Many of the students there did not have their drivers' licenses nor did they know how to drive. Apparently, during the Depression, many families did without cars entirely, relying instead on bicycles, public transport, or foot traffic. I, on the other hand, had grown up on a farm where machinery was a way of life. From a very young age I had been a driver of tractors, trucks, and automobiles. This experience enabled me to graduate at the top of the class.

The top three of us were called into the commandant's office where we were offered the opportunity to go to Officer Candidate School (OCS). I immediately declined being unable to get used to the idea of being an undersized Lieutenant wading around in three feet of snow in Germany, trying to command troops, all of whom would likely be larger than I was. I still had a strong desire to fly, and if I accepted this offer that would not be happening. I stayed with my dream.

Chapter Five: A New Place and a New Job

Within a week I was called back to the commander's office and given a new assignment. I was to report to a Signal Corps detachment at Kern County Airport near Bakersfield, California. The commanding officer there, seeing my driving school records, appointed me as his personal driver. It was a very cushy job since my entire duty schedule revolved around my commander's need to be driven from place to place, which did not always need to be done. I was told to stay available to him at any time so that he could freely move about. In order to be free at any moment, I was allowed to skip many of the usual duties assigned to every other enlisted man on the base. I never stood inspection or cleaned a kitchen as long as I was there. I was even able to earn extra money driving a dump truck for a man who owned a gravel pit nearby. All in all, things could have been worse.

Due to this fortunate placement, I first came into contact with the P-38 Lightning. There, four flying sergeants based at nearby Muroc Field were allowed to land at Kern County Field so they could go home on weekends. I watched these magnificent machines come into the base and was fascinated by them. I had no idea what I was looking at, but I was determined to find out. I asked a nearby soldier what those planes were, and he told me they were P-38 fighters. I stood for a moment and once again proclaimed aloud to those nearby that I would one day fly that plane.

After a couple of months my commanding officer sent me on an errand to Minter Field where I happened upon a building with a small sign on the front reading "Air Corps Exams."

Upon completing my assigned duties, I drove the command car over to that building and sought further information. I found an officer standing on the porch smoking a cigarette, and I saluted him properly and told him I was there to see about the Air Corps Examination. Neglecting to ask me for identification and orders, he directed me to a sergeant inside the office. I told the sergeant that his commanding officer had sent me in to see about the Air Corps exam. This white lie got me papers to fill out that I completed quickly and when I handed them back, he gave me the booklet containing the exam I wanted. He directed me to a side room where I found six other servicemen engaged in taking the test. I joined them and set to work.

After approximately two hours and forty-five minutes I had completed the exam and turned it in. After that I returned to Kern County Airport.

For several days thereafter I maintained a very low profile hoping to escape attention until my results arrived. Since I had acted on my own initiative, outside of the chain of command, I was likely to catch an earful at least when things finally developed. I waited several days without information. It was pins and needles time.

During the second week of waiting I was summoned to the commander's office. I reported promptly and came to attention offering a crisp salute upon entering his office. The chief was looking at a sheaf of paper in his hand and seemed not to notice me. When he at last looked up and did not return my salute, I knew I was in for it, front and center.

For the next several minutes I caught Holy Ned for embarrassing the captain's authority, stepping outside of the chain of command, and several other things I would hate to mention. I even heard about the dump truck. Finally the skipper seemed to calm himself a bit, and soon the royal chew out was over. After a brief pause, the chief actually smiled at me. "Behrns," he said, "very few people take the Air Corps test cold turkey and pass it. You did that and you passed high. Congratulations, son. You are now in the Air Corps."

With that he offered me his hand, which I took. Shaking that hand at that moment was the only thing that kept me from flying right out of the room.

BOOK TWO: The Air Corps

Chapter Six: Another Detour — The Signal Corps

From Kern County Airport, I was given orders to report to Santa Ana to join an Air Corps unit. There was a gap between assignments, and I found myself with leave to go home for a few days before reporting to my next duty station. I really didn't need any rest, but it was good the see friends and family again.

At Santa Ana the military routine changed completely. Regimentation was extremely tight, much more so than any I had previously experienced. A whistle blew at 5:30 a.m., and our feet hit the floor immediately. First we made our beds to military specifications, which meant the inspector coming through could bounce a quarter off the surface and catch it. Then we moved into the "four S" routine. The first "S" was a bathroom stop. We had to condition ourselves to accomplish this by the clock since there would be no other opportunity during the morning to answer a call of nature. It was 'get it done early or hold it all day.' Next we would shave and then hit the shower. After those two "S's," we dressed for the day's activities and carefully shined our shoes. With our "S" routine completed, we would fall-in, in front of the barracks, and march to the mess hall for breakfast using precision marching techniques including the squarest of turns.

When we entered the building, we found long tables where our breakfast was laid out on large platters. We marched forward until a leader reached the end of the seating bench. At that point the drill instructor called a halt. The next command was "LEFT FACE," and we all turned to face the table. On command, we seated ourselves and began to fill our plates. All moves, including those made with either knife or fork, were made in square configuration. The fork went out, stopped, moved straight down for a bite, moved back vertically, still extended and finally came to our mouths in a straight line. We must have looked like Santa Claus' wooden soldiers as we ate. Fortunately, the food was terrific, and we really didn't mind.

When the allotted time for eating was over, the sergeant again blew his whistle, and everything immediately stopped. If you had a fork full of dessert on the way up you had to return it to the plate, still using square, vertical movements before the order to rise came and the unit moved out to begin the day's drills.

Next, we went through a period of calisthenics and running, followed by close-order drills. We put in about an hour in this fashion before moving into classroom for daily instruction. The first period was math. On the first day the instructor went to the board at the front of the class and wrote one plus one in chalk for everyone to see. Then he turned to the class and gestured for an answer. Answers were forthcoming but were nowhere near consistent. Perhaps some did not see the plus sign on the vertically arranged problem. Most of us called out the correct answer of "two," but here and there I could hear "one" and "zero." Apparently this was not unusual because the instructor did not seem at all surprised by the variety of responses. He smiled and nodded and then moved quickly on. By afternoon we were deep into algebra.

At noon we formed up into our group and precision-marched back to the mess hall where we observed the same careful square-angled routine we had followed in the morning. After lunch it was back to the classroom. We had to learn Morse code, which I thoroughly detested. Never in my career did I have occasion to use the stuff. I none-the-less learned it. Shortly thereafter I dismissed it from my mind and felt no loss at all.

We next returned to the mess hall for our supper and then to the barracks where we invariably had one to two hours of homework per night. At ten o'clock sharp, the whistle blew for lights out, and our day was ended. The reason for the precise nature of our routine was to instill discipline deeply into our behavior. The Air Corps believed that discipline and orderly behavior could mean the difference between life and death on the battlefield or in the air. Under extreme stress the soldier reverts to training, and proper training will help him 'soldier through' to fight another day. Over the years I was to see the truth of this many times. At the moment, however, it was merely a daily grind.

At the end of three months we were transferred north to Santa Maria, California, to attend Allan Hancock College of Aeronautics. Two hundred of us came to Santa Maria by train and arrived at our destination at one o'clock in the morning. Captain G. Allan Hancock, the oil company magnate and owner of the school, met us on the train, decked out in a correct train engineer's suit including the tall hat, gloves, overalls—the works. He told us that early morning we were in for a real workout, and only five of every one hundred who came to school would ever graduate and fly the plane of their choice. That worried me more than a little bit at that moment. I estimated my chances as rather low considering the numbers and talent surrounding me. But, I had come this far, and the goal lay ahead, so I got to it with gusto.

We had several days of ground school, and then I was introduced to my instructor, Mr. Caradies, who was a large man and a civilian. He sat me down and explained that the only things I needed to know to fly an airplane were how to take it up off the ground and how to safely bring it back onto the ground. All of the other skills of flying would be learned later. The next day would be my orientation flight.

He first took me to the parachute shop where we watched chutes being packed. He then explained the use of this primary safety device and the methods of deploying one when needed. He then picked up a parachute and told me to bring one. We walked from there out to the plane we would use the next morning, an open-cockpit Stearman biplane, built by the Boeing company of Seattle, Washington, called by the Air Corps a PT-19.

My first airplane-based lesson proved to be how to do a pre-flight check, which was accomplished by walking slowly around the craft looking at all critical parts. This inspection included checking the control surfaces for damage and for freedom of movement, which I found was done by physically moving the elevators, ailerons, and vertical stabilizer with your hands. I was now ready for my first flight.

That night reality set in as I realized how close I was to my goal of becoming a pilot. No sleep.

Hancock training plane (Bill Behrns' collection)

Chapter Seven: Into The Air

The next morning I met Mr. Caradies at the plane, and he helped me climb into the cockpit and secure myself. This was entirely new ground for me since I had never been in an airplane before, much less ridden in one. We went through basic seatbelt procedures, and he began the task of making me familiar with the interior of the small space I now inhabited. He then climbed into the rear cockpit, and we went through startup. The crewman cranked the inertial starter until proper rpm's were reached at which time Mr. Caradies would holler, "Fore," and everyone nearby cleared out. Then the instructor closed the ignition, and the crewman engaged the clutch. This was greeted with a throaty roar as the engine fired up and gained speed, spinning the prop happily. Just like that we

Instrument display on Stearman trainer (Bill Behrns' collection)

were moving. My head and shoulders were above the sides of the cockpit while a small windscreen protected my eyes from the prop wash. My helmet and goggles protected me from any other problems associated with airflow. There was no radio equipment in our training planes. Communication with my instructor was accomplished by means of a speaking tube, which ran from the front cockpit to the rear seat where Mr. Caradies sat. It was a one-way line from him to me. I could hear him talk, but there was no way to reply vocally. I could hear him talk, but acknowledge commands or indicate if I had a question. The system was crude but effective.

We moved down the runway with me following his control by feel, my hands and feet lightly on the controls to get a sense of what Mr. Caradies was feeding into the control surfaces as we gained speed. In a few moments we broke free from the ground, and I had a feeling of euphoria as I realized I was actually flying. One more step achieved, but there was no time to think about it. We were gaining altitude rapidly, and new things were on the way.

Training runway at Hancock Field (Bill Behrns' collection)

At approximately three thousand feet, Mr. Caradies leveled off, came on the speaker tube, and asked if I was firmly strapped in. I gave the visual signal for yes, and he immediately did a half snap, inverting the plane. At that instant I thought I was leaving the airplane. Where the space between me and the seat came from I'll never know, but it was very suddenly there. It was a moment of stark terror as I seemed to be dangling from my seat belt with inches of room beneath me. Would I stop in time? Was I going to fall? The strange feeling in the pit of my stomach was even stranger upside down. Eventually my instructor righted the aircraft. After a few seconds he came on the speaker tube and said, "Now, Mister, are you properly strapped in?"

I had nearly cut myself in two tightening the strap with quaking hands. I again raised my hand "yes," albeit more slowly. Lesson learned. More to come.

Mr. Caradies then proceeded to demonstrate a series of maneuvers I would be expected to learn. I became somewhat nauseated but was fortunately able to contain my reactions, so that I did not cause my teacher any concern. I would later discover that some of the students had been less able to withstand the stress and had thrown up inside their cockpits. On landing they were ordered to clean up the plane, which was no fun at all.

When we returned to the field I once again lightly followed my instructor's movements as he easily touched down and taxied to a stop. My first day in the air was at an end.

The next morning I followed Mr. Caradies' control of the plane by lightly feeling his moves with the stick and the pedals. We made one pass over the field and then gently landed, promptly taking off again to make another pass and once more land. We did this all morning, with him flying and me shadowing his moves until I began to gain an understanding of what was needed to make the aircraft do what I would soon want from it. We continued with these "touch and go" landings for a full three hours before we finished for the day. I had done no real flying on my own, but I was thoroughly worn out.

The next morning we repeated the process, doing one touch and go takeoff and landing after another. Each time I would place my hands gently on the controls and follow my instructor's lead as we went on and off the field. As the time moved on, we finished day two without incident, and I knew I was making progress. Now, how much longer before I could fly alone? We would soon see.

Strearman bi-plane used at Hancock Aviation Academy
(Bill Behrns' collection)

Chapter Eight: Solo

The third day of instruction began, as had the previous two with Mr. Caradies and I doing more touch and go landings on the Hancock strip. As we continued training I was feeling more and more confident in my ability to handle the aircraft in these simple but necessary maneuvers. I was beginning to feel quite good about the situation in general. One hour into the day things abruptly changed.

As we landed Mr. Caradies ordered me to stop the plane, which I did. He climbed out of the rear cockpit and proceeded straight to the ground. He then moved forward to be even with my cockpit, pointed a finger at me, and said in a loud voice, "Mister," as cadets were called, "you're probably going to kill somebody some day, but you are not going to kill me today. GET GOING!"

He swung his arm forward pointing down the runway and turned and walked away from the plane leaving me in sole possession of the Stearman. Another moment of terror had arrived. It was time to solo right then and there.

I fed in power and started down the runway intending to take off and instead I found myself drifting rapidly off line, to the left. I had neglected to correct for the torque of the engine, which is counteracted with the right rudder pedal. The condition is called "Yaw," and I was in one. I fed in correction and promptly began drifting to the right. I had overcorrected. Back I went to the left, and once more I went too far. Coming back right I anticipated properly and got myself straight. Try as I might I don't recall picking up the tail but I must have because a few seconds later, I looked down and found myself twenty or so feet in the air. A feeling of exaltation swept over me as I looked around and realized that momma Behrns' little boy Bill was actually flying an airplane. I was really doing what I had always wanted to do. I was flying. The next moment of terror was only moments away as I realized I had to get back down.

I circled the field and put myself back into the landing pattern, turning on final approach and heading for the runway. So far, so good. I was gaining confidence by the second. Everything appeared to be right as I flared the plane for stall onto the runway. Unfortunately, instead of being six inches off the asphalt as I had planned, I was three feet above the pavement. I came down hard with an audible *thud*, bounded back into the air, and tried to recover my plane and my composure. Two more bounces and I was back on terra firma. Mr. Caradies had apparently expected this and motioned me onward for another try. He then walked off the runway to watch from a distance.

The next time around was better but still a bit rough. I didn't hit quite so hard, but I still wasn't smooth. Several more tries and I got it right, or nearly so. After a while, Mr. Caradies

Stearman bi-plane student trainer
(Bill Behrns' collection)

was satisfied and motioned me to the side of the runway. I taxied to the parking area, shut down the Stearman and made my way to the ground.

Mr. Caradies

came up and shook hands with me. He then congratulated me and presented me with my signed solo certificate that completed my early instruction. It was the first certificate awarded to any member of that class. I was a pilot.

Chapter Nine: Early Flight School

We remained at the Hancock Academy for three more weeks, learning how to do the aerobatic maneuvers a pilot needed to know in order to keep himself alive in combat, assuming we progressed that far. We spent three hours each morning in our "space" moving the plane in various loops, circles, dives, turns, rolls, stalls, and so forth until we knew what could and could not be done with our bi-planes. Each of us had our own "space" in the air and a definite technique for locating it. We were instructed to fly out for several minutes away from base, each on a different heading and assigned altitude. We were then to locate a stationary point on the ground to use as a reference point for our place in the air. Then we would develop an area half a mile on each side, half a mile below, and half a mile above. That box of air was our assigned station in which we could work with our planes and learn their limits. We tried just about every aerobatic move we could think of, and thanks to the ever-forgiving Stearman trainers, we survived our mistakes and practiced until we could do most everything within the flight envelope of that plane. I built up about 80 hours of flight time before the next assignment landed in front of me.

One incident from our on-station time was particularly interesting. We had no radios in our trainers so communications were simple and direct. The control tower had a powerful, laser-like light, green in color, with which they could summon a particular plane to return to base. Controllers focused the concentrated beam on a pilot's face so that he could not miss seeing it. Nearby pilots could not see the light until it was intended for them. On this day, shortly after arrival on station, members began to be recalled to base. The last plane out was the first called back. A powerful windstorm had come up making it necessary to retrieve the planes quickly. I noticed this action but was not aware of a reason since the air around my station was reasonably calm.

Since I was the first plane out every morning, for reasons I never was able to determine, I was the last plane to be called back to base. Upon arriving over Hancock Field I could see a lot of dust flying about and several clumps of dust swirling near the ground. On approach to the runway my plane was drifting south of my objective causing me to correct my trajectory north to compensate. The wind-shear factor was causing the wind-direction marker, known as the "T," to move about unpredictably. I was unable to line up directly on it, as I was supposed to, landing instead at an angle slightly north of parallel. I managed to land safely and felt pretty good about it until Mr. Caradies reminded me that I was supposed to land as the "T" indicated. He then went on to quietly congratulate me for getting down safely since 14 other pilots had ground-looped on landing, several of them damaging their planes. Mine was safe and sound in spite of landing under the toughest conditions. All in all things could have been worse.

Our class graduated from Hancock College of Aeronautics on February 5, 1943, after which I would move on to another duty station. I had reached my initial goal of becoming a pilot and flying like Roscoe Turner and Tex Rankin. I had, however, adjusted my sight upward since that first decision. I had seen a P-38, and I wanted one. My next stop would be on a field where intermediate trainers would lead us to real fighter planes. I was making progress.

Chapter Ten: Basic Flight Training

From Santa Maria, I went to Merced County Airport, later to be called Castle Air Force Base. There I was assigned to fly the Consolidated Vultee BT-13 (basic trainer). Nicknamed the "Valiant" by Consolidated, the plane soon came by another name given it by the pilots who flew it. The plane had a tendency to shake and shimmy at higher speeds—"Vibrator," the flyers called it.

The BT-13 was a low-wing, closed-cockpit monoplane with a 450-horsepower Pratt and Whitney radial engine for power. With twice the horsepower of the Stearman, the Vibrator had considerably more speed and performance. As pilots, we had to adjust our timing and extend our awareness to take in the shorter response times called for by the new level of performance.

Another feature of this plane was the unusual shape of the canopy. The long and somewhat narrow "greenhouse" enclosure provided room for both pilot and instructor with dual controls and instruments. The crown of our little house on the airplane did not rise into a smooth arc above the pilot's head as most such covers did. The Vibrator lid narrowed at the top into a pyramid-like shape which left just enough room for the pilot's head and very little else. I would soon become very familiar with this interesting design.

After studying cockpit procedure and taking a couple of flights with an instructor, I felt quite comfortable in the new configuration. It was an easy transition and after the first week, my training flights were nearly all solo. Once in a while an instructor would come along to monitor my progress but for the most part it was an exercise in gaining hours and experience in a predictable plane.

One morning my instructor told me to go up and practice some aerobatics and then to work on stall and spin recovery. This latter assignment had been a simple thing in Stearman which would allow the pilot to recover from a spin at almost any point, simply by applying power and flying out of it. In a Vibrator it was an entirely different game. First I had to bring the plane to stall by lifting the nose without adding power until the plane reached zero air speed and stopped flying. Then I would drop the nose and push the stick forward while neutralizing the rudders, putting the plane into a moderate dive, picking up speed before pulling out and flying once again. This was easy enough, but there was more to do to induce a spin. The plane would stall and I would reverse controls at that precise moment. Full left rudder, stick full right, and full back position and I was in a spin—next lesson coming up fast.

In a BT-13, recovery from a spin should commence immediately, or the plane began to have a mind of its own. The Vibrator would go into a violent "snap" spin, increasing in speed with each revolution. If allowed to continue, the wings could soon come off the plane. This was to be avoided at all costs if the pilot wished to live to fly tomorrow. I found this out the hard way by neglecting to begin early recovery and allowing the first "snap" to occur before I got myself together and started flying again. Naturally, there was a price to pay.

I made my stall-move above five thousand feet to allow room to fall "comfortably" so that I would not have to do anything too quickly. With that in mind I was entirely too casual about regaining control after inducing a spin. I allowed the BT-13 to come around without slowing the turn, and the BT-13 did exactly what my instructor and the training manual said it would do, it gained speed in the turn and went into a sharp "snap" spin which caught me completely off-guard. As my plane whipped suddenly right, I hit my head on the narrow canopy, hard enough to make me see stars. I corrected quickly, too quickly, and promptly hit the other side of my head on the opposite side of the very narrow canopy. More stars and an audible groan! I had just had my ears boxed! I remembered well what my mother would say after she boxed my ears (so much more gently) after I had misbehaved at home. "Bill, don't do that again," she would say to me, sternly. I recalled her words as I pulled out of the spin and went back to altitude to try it again. This time I induced the spin and corrected immediately, avoiding contact with the Plexiglas roof under which I sat.

I soon finished my practice schedule and returned to base. There I confessed my sins to my instructor who had a good laugh over it all, especially when I explained how I had boxed my ears and remembered Mother doing the same thing to me at home. "And what do you say now that your plane has boxed your ears?" he asked me, grinning hugely.

"I'll say I won't do that again," I replied.

"Your mother is a wise lady," he said. "Enough for today. Tomorrow, more work."

And so it was until the next challenge, which proved to be night flying.

Chapter Eleven: Night Flying

None of the cadets in my class had ever attempted to fly at night so our next training regimen was completely new to all of us. Our instructors described to us what they expected us to do, but their instructions did not come close to the actual difficulty of the task ahead. First we were trucked out to a huge ranch a few miles west of Merced County Airport where there was a private runway set up at a place called Potter Field. There were three BT-13 trainers sitting next to the field for us to use.

Vultee BT-13 "Vibrator" (photo by Ken Moore)

At the approach end of the runway there were orange crates set up, vertically, side-by-side, upon which was placed a small battery-powered lantern, which could be seen from some distance. Directly across the runway was another identical setup. On approach we had to land between and beyond these markers. To be sure we were not short of our goal, a string was run across the runway, orange-crate high. About 120 feet farther up the strip, the same setup was duplicated with another string running between the crates. We were to catch this string with our landing gear as we passed it, marking our landing points within the allowed space. We had to be firmly on the ground before contacting the second string or the landing would not count.

After full darkness, our training began, and the unanticipated problem reared its ugly head. There was no moon out at that time of the month and no other light at all in the neighborhood of Potter Field. Once off the ground I experienced the weird sensation of having absolutely no idea where my horizon was. Without this necessary frame of reference, a pilot has no visual resources. Since we were not yet fully instrument trained, I was suddenly at a loss to know just where it was I was flying my airplane. I could have been climbing or diving for all of the information I had coming to me. I really needed some visual reference point, but try as I might, I could not find one. Finally, in the distance, I saw a faint stationary light, which came from a small farm some miles north of me. I was able fix upon that spot of brightness and use it as a makeshift North Star. I had my horizon, and I adjusted my pitch and vector in reference to it. From here on I knew where I was and completed the first turn in good order. I cleared the first string barrier and set down safely before the second. I then lifted off, completing my first touch and go, and swung around for another pass.

There was a moment's discomfort when I failed to find my little light immediately, but soon enough I located it and came in for my second successful pass. All in all, each of us made a half-dozen passes through the course before retiring for the night. All of us completed the exercise successfully.

It was a rather exciting night for a night-flying beginner, probably the scariest moment I had encountered in my brief experience with airplanes. I would grow quite comfortable with night flying as the days went on until a full week of night landings were under my belts. After completing and passing my check rides, my Basic Training was over, and I was ready for Advanced Training. I was assigned to a new duty station at Williams Field in Arizona. I picked up a classmate in Bakersfield and drove the two of us to Tempe, Arizona, for the next phase.

Chapter Twelve: Advanced Training

At Williams, I began my training in a Curtis AT-9. This aircraft was my first twin-engine ride, and there was a good deal to learn. First of all a pilot was suddenly confronted with twice as many instruments as he was used to in the single-engine planes of earlier training. The AT-9 had twin, 295-horsepower Lycoming engines, which would drive the plane forward at 110 miles per hour cruising. In all honesty the Boeing did almost everything at 110 miles per hour. Takeoff was at 110 miles per hour, as was cruising, as was landing. The lack of variety was amazing. The ride could have been down-right boring except for the fact that a pilot needed to stay on high alert at all times in an AT-9. The plane had a nasty habit of reminding new pilots just how new they really were by magnifying mistakes and being less than forgiving about them when it did. An AT-9 could kill you in a hurry if you didn't watch it very carefully.

We were instructed early on to keep one eye on the ground at all times while flying the Curtis trainer. Engine failure could overtake you quickly, and there might well be need of a place to land safely away from our home field in that event. One day I was scoping out places to put my plane in an emergency when my instructor quietly shut off the fuel supply to both engines simultaneously which caused sudden and complete engine failure. Unaware of the reason for loss of power, I hurriedly sought out a field or pasture or country road on which I could land my oversized glider. I was losing altitude quickly and finding no relief. We got down to about seventy-five feet above ground without a landing spot when the instructor abruptly turned the fuel back on and the wind-milling engines restarted, enabling me to regain altitude and allow myself a sigh of relief. This intensely realistic piece of safety training made a big impression on young pilot Bill, and after that moment, I always had a point of relief in the back of my mind.

Years later I met an instructor pilot who had over 400 hours in the AT-9. Glen Vanderford told me about his time at Douglas Field. "I dearly loved that airplane," he said to me. "As a pilot I wouldn't have cared much for it, but as an instructor it was a great ride. It made the student concentrate on his tasks because inattention could get you in trouble fast. It was also the best plane the Air Corps had for teaching instrument flying. After the AT-9, a young pilot really knew his way around instruments."

After completing initial training in the AT-9, I was initiated into the Institute of the Blind, otherwise known as instrument training. Instrument was conducted in a mock-up cockpit mounted on a pedestal. This was called a Link Trainer, and it contained a complete set of controls and instruments necessary for blind flying. The trainer was encased in a black-out cover, which allowed no light to find its way inside. All interior illumination was provided by the soft glow of the instruments.

Outside on the pedestal was an alternate control panel with complete overriding control of everything inside of the Link Trainer. This control system could create cloud cover, storms, high winds, and just about everything else your plane was likely to encounter in any attitude in which the plane might find itself. The station was manned by a sergeant whom we came to believe was sadistic, crazy, alcoholic, or all three. That guy could and did throw some amazingly difficult combinations of conditions at us in increasingly difficult stages as our hours in the trainer began to build up. Our duty was to defeat the sergeant's imagination by overcoming and correcting each situation while flying blind, thereby avoiding simulated crashes and the embarrassment that went with them. Everybody crashed at one time or another until we learned to keep the needle and ball within the norms. Wind shear was probably the nastiest problem 'Sarge' could throw at us. It was nearly instantaneous and had to be countered correctly and immediately or you were in a simulated disaster right then and there. The experience was intense and formative. All in all, the Link Trainer was one of the really valuable training regimens we went through. We learned to rely on those gauges and dials as if there was nothing else because there really was nothing else. We further learned to trust those instruments completely. This was real lifesaving training, and I would come to appreciate it later on.

Upon satisfactory completion of the course and the obligatory tests that followed, I earned my certificate of graduation from the Institute of the Blind. Next would be my introduction to the Cessna AT-17, unaffectionately known as the "Bamboo Bomber."

AT-17 (Bill Behrns' collection)

At Williams Field, the Bamboo Bomber was used as a vehicle for us to put our instrument training into practice in a real aircraft. It was equipped with a special hood over the pilot's seat while the instructor sat in the right-hand seat, which was in the open, as normal. Flying blind, on instruments only over a preplanned route, each pilot would complete a routine previously presented to his instructor. My instructor was very helpful and helped me plan a routine, which could be used by a higher officer on a check ride. We took an AT-17 to the end of the runway and parked a few yards off the surface at a forty-five degree angle. I then released the brakes and moved at idle to the center of the runway, which we had previously determined through practice, by using the clock to tell me where I was. Then I turned onto the proper heading, advanced the throttles and became airborne, watching the clock all of the way. I held a constant rate of climb until I reached five hundred feet, whereupon I made a ninety-degree turn retaining my rate of climb and keeping the ball in the socket as assigned. Then, continuing the rate of climb, I rose to seven hundred feet altitude and, when the clock was right, turned ninety degrees to the left. I continued my climb until I reached one thousand feet, ever mindful of the constantly moving hands on the clock. There I leveled off and made a left turn, ninety degrees and continued, knowing the elapsed time to my next ninety degree turn. At the completion of this routine I should be, in theory, lined-up for approach on my original runway.

Now, still flying blind, I made that last turn, beginning at one thousand feet, and descended to the runway just as if I knew what I was doing the entire way, which I soon discovered I actually did. I had trusted my instruments completely, and they had delivered me spot-on to my destination. Wow!

Later my instructor would tell me that my plan was a very ambitious one for a check-ride, but he saw no reason why I should change one thing about it. I didn't.

My check-ride came up immediately that same day. I waited in the ready-room and shortly a major walked in. He proved to be a man of few words, saying simply, "Behrns," (statement, not question). I jumped up and saluted him, and he asked me if I had my routine. I said "Yes, sir," and handed him my clipboard. He looked at it briefly and said, "Let's go." He turned and went out the door with me close behind.

We entered my plane, and he pulled the hood over my head and asked me if I was ready to begin. I started the engines, and then performed the entire routine just as I had practiced it with my instructor. On approach to the field for final landing, when I reached an altitude of less than thirty feet, the major reached over and pulled my hood back, and I was suddenly in full sunlight, sitting directly over my runway. I landed smoothly and taxied to a parking area. There we got out of the aircraft. He wrote a few words on the bottom of his board and handed it to me. There I found two columns, each for every maneuver I had made. One column was labeled PASS and the other was labeled FAIL. One would not want to see too many checks on the FAIL side, and I was pleased by what I saw. The Major had checked every single move as PASS and on the bottom summary was just one word. PASSED. Next to that in parenthesis was one more word, EXCELLENT! I suddenly liked this man! Our final exchange was just as brief as everything else. He said to me "Congratulations," and turned and walked away

My instructor was waiting for me off to the side of the parking area, sitting in his jeep. He took my clipboard from me, looked it over and said, "Congratulations, hop in."

I did, and we rode about a mile down the line where we found several P-322s. This Lockheed plane was a forerunner of the P-38, being a good copy, with counter-rotating props but without the power-giving turbo superchargers.

"Climb into that bird right there," he said, "and learn the instrumentation and control setup. When you have it figured out, let me know."

I climbed out of the jeep. He drove off, heading for the operations building and leaving me behind. I walked over to the impressive aircraft in front of me and found my way to the rear of the gondola where I mounted the built-in ladder and climbed into the cockpit. The 322, sometimes called a Castrated Lightning, was a single-seat plane. There was no instructor in there with me. I was alone in a fighter plane.

Chapter Thirteen: The 322 and Beyond

The sight of those Lockheed 322 trainers was a thing of beauty. The plane looked very much like her big sister, the P-38 Lightning and was used as a transition platform from the AT-17 Bamboo Bomber to the combat-ready Lightning. The 322 had the slim, linear silhouette that caused people to remember this unique Lockheed airframe. As I sat in the jeep with my instructor on that fine valley morning, I remember being struck by the fact that this aircraft looked fast just sitting on the ground. She seemed to lean eagerly forward on her tricycle landing gear as if anxious to be off and flying. I could hardly wait to climb into one and fly off. But wait I would, because I had homework to do.

My instructor ordered me to do a ground check and then get into the cockpit and make myself at home until I knew the place. Then I was to thoroughly read the instruction manual provided by Lockheed, and when I felt comfortable with the instruments and characteristics, I should mount up, crank the engines, taxi a few times, and take off. This would once again be a touch and go session, which had been a hallmark of our training since Hancock Field.

I began as I was instructed and fired up the 322. My exuberance at this point must have reached the sky. I felt at home and pumped up at the same time. I noticed several things at once that were important differences in this airplane from anything else I had flown to date. First of all was my unobstructed view of the field. In a tail dragger, I could never look directly ahead until I had enough speed to raise the tail off the ground. Before that, any pilot had to look left or right because the engine cowl was directly and hugely in front. To see ahead, the pilot would weave back and forth across the taxi-way to avoid running over whatever could not be seen beneath his prop. The 322 had no such limitation. The tricycle landing gear gave this plane a horizontal platform upon which to taxi. I could see everything! Wonderful!

Beyond that, the counter-rotating props completely eliminated the necessity to correct for engine torque. The 322 taxied with all of the ease of a passenger car. I simply pointed the nose forward and went right to where I wanted to go. It couldn't be this easy, but it was. I taxied back and forth a few times until I felt confident enough to take off and fly. I moved to the end of the runway and, with permission from the tower, I rolled out and poured the coal to my eager plane. The 322 seemed to jump into the air and head for the clouds almost by itself. The plane seemed an eager stallion, and I was very ready to ride.

I cycled the landing gear to clean up the air-flow and settled in for one of the most enjoyable rides I had ever experienced. The plane handled wonderfully. Without the constant need to correct for torque, I found it simple to pick a spot in the air and be there almost immediately. What performance! The platform was very steady and predictable. The cockpit sat high and above most other parts of the plane, allowing me to look about and see the air and ground around me. The only place I could not see well was at an angle slightly behind my seat. Straight behind was available through a rearview mirror, which was adequate but not terrific. The day would come, a year or two later in combat, when that mirror would save my life.

One additional blind-spot was caused by the protruding engine nacelles on either side of the plane. The air below

Cockpit of the Lockheed Type 322 (photo by Ken Moore)

the engines was hard to see but tipping the plane from side to side could provide the necessary view. All in all, the 322 provided a better look at the sky than I had ever experienced before.

I swung around the landing field and began the routine of touch and go, familiarizing myself with the takeoff and landing characteristics of the trainer. The old saying from Mr. Caradies was still true. You must take off and land before you attempt to do anything else. Once again the tricycle landing proved its worth since everything was visible in front at all times. The 322 was a breeze to land. It was smooth and almost gentle. Ground visibility allowed a pilot to know the instant his wheels would touch, and I found it possible to touch wheels lightly and "grease" a landing much more easily than I had ever done before. Up to that moment, landing had not been my strongest suit, but the tricycle gear allowed me to improve my technique rapidly. Landings became much more fun. No more bounces.

We were taught to hold the nose-wheel slightly high and land on the main gear, waiting about forty yards before letting down the nose. This kept us from damaging the front strut with too heavy an impact. Touchdown occurred at 90 miles per hour and then slowdown commenced.

There was one other area where a bit of concern could enter a pilot's day. The brakes on the 322, and also on P-38, were just barely adequate to stop the plane within the confines of most runways. Small fields were not good places to land. Constant pressure on the brake system did little good. There was no constant-pressure master cylinder on the airplane so it was necessary to pump the brakes regularly to maintain necessary pressure for proper brake performance. Twin-engine power was preciously close to overwhelming technology, and pilot technique became vital to the equation. Training at this performance level was more intense and for good reason.

I flew the 322 for four days, and my instructor was happy with my progress. On the afternoon of the fourth day, he took me another half mile down the taxiway, and there we found several full-blown P-38s. A few students were working out in the big fighters, getting in the required hours for qualification. There was no transition necessary this time since the difference between the 322 and the P-38 was primarily horsepower. The Lightnings had twenty-five hundred horses available with turbocharger assist, and they were the hot-rods of the Air Corps. This was the warhorse I said I would ride if I could make it to combat, and I was ready to ride that horse as soon as I could mount up on one.

An officer assigned me to an airplane and I stood practically pawing the ground until my chosen craft became available. I walked around my new chariot performing a thorough and careful ground check, all of the time admiring the state-of-the art engineering before me. I then climbed up the built-in rear ladder, retracting it when I reached the wing. It was a routine I would perform hundreds of times over the years, but that afternoon it was a very special thing. I walked up the wing, watching where I put my feet, and stepped into the cockpit.

The taxi and takeoff procedures were familiar from my time in the 322 so I felt comfortable as I strapped myself into my first Lightning. I was where I had wanted to be since the first time I had seen one of these planes back at Kern County Airport. All I needed to do was take off and land to achieve my next goal. It was an amazing thing to think about, but I soon found out that reality was so much better. Never had I been so ready to fly.

Chapter Fourteen: Flying the Lightning

I ran through my mental checklist as I looked around the cockpit and felt the controls for response. Everything was in order, and I was ready to commence the flight of my dreams. I took a moment to consider my situation before I initiated engine start. Not many people actually get to do the things they most want in life, but young Bill Behrns was about to undertake one of the really big ones.

I took a deep breath and let it out slowly, helping myself to relax a bit, and engaged the starter on the left-hand engine where the electric generator was. This was the recommended procedure since there would be more power for the remaining operations with the generator turning over, providing fresh electricity for everything else. The big Allison engine turned over three times and fired up. I then turned my attention to the right-side engine and repeated the process with similar results. My heart was pounding away beneath my shirt as I moved my feet on and off the brake pedals to keep the plane stationary while I chose a path to the edge of the runway where I could perform my run-up before takeoff. I lifted my right foot and allowed the plane to pivot on the left wheel while the right rolled. In that manner I performed a nearly square turn that pointed me toward the runway. A little left throttle facilitated the move and put me on the right track. I taxied to the entry point on the run-up zone and braked to a stop. I sat there for about three minutes, massaging the brakes and warming up the twin Allisons. I checked the magnetos and the engine temperatures and found both satisfactory. Next were the controls for the Curtis Electric Propellers. Was the pitch correct on each and could I get the props to respond? So far, so good on all things.

I taxied onto the runway and moved forward a few feet to be certain of a straight line for takeoff. It was critical to have the nose-wheel straight ahead, and I determined that mine was aligned properly. Then I pumped and set the brakes before powering up. I set the throttles forward to full military power and engine revolutions to 3,000 rpm. Then I set the turbo-superchargers to 50-plus inches of mercury. Under this strong "boost" the plane was straining against the brakes as if yearning to go forward. My bird wanted to fly.

On release of the brakes there was a sudden surge, which pushed me back into my seat. The plane gained speed more quickly than anything I had been in before and within five or six hundred feet I had achieved a speed of nearly one hundred and thirty miles per hour. At that point I lifted the nose and allowed my plane to break free from the ground and climb into the air. Within seconds I had cycled the landing gear and was above 190 miles per hour. I was flying the Lightning and enjoying the feeling of pure power I had in my hands. The big fighter gained speed rapidly and was soon above 250 miles per hour. I was wishing I could go for more, but the limitations of touch and go intruded upon the feeling of freedom, and I was quickly back on task.

My first flight contained several touch and go executions before I came down and parked the big, wonderful fighter plane I had so long dreamed about. I moved to the parking area, shut down the engines and sat for a few moments, thoroughly pleased with the events of the day. The dream was at hand, and I intended to extend it out as far as I possibly could. I dismounted from the plane and walked back to the parking area to catch a six-by-six ride back to the squadron orderly room before returning to barracks. The big, canvass-covered, two and a half-ton trucks would be our conveyance to and from our barracks each day. We followed this routine daily as part of our regular training.

After the morning flight there were some studies and tasks to complete before we were on our own. The fun part came when we were allowed to return to the flight line and "check out" a P-38 unofficially and go out and fly for the pure joy and experience of it. There were three of us who showed up every day for those extra flights, which did not officially exist. We nicknamed ourselves the Gung Ho's because of our intense love of flying, particularly in those P-38s. We took them out whenever the officer-in-charge would let us. On these excursions we would fly up over Phoenix at approximately ten thousand feet, switch our radios to local stations and listen to the modern dance bands of that day while we flew

Early P-38 dashboard (photo courtesy of P-38 National Association)

our fighters. Glen Miller, Benny Goodman, and Harry James were all favorites of ours. We used to perform aerobatic maneuvers to the music, seeing if we could complete a loop or a roll at the end of a measure or section. There was a certain rhythm to all of it, and we spent considerable time searching for it.

There were also huge, white, fluffy cumulous clouds to play with. One at a time we would approach a cloud. We would then invert our craft and fly into white oblivion with our hands and feet completely off the controls. In a few seconds we would come out the far side without knowing exactly what attitude we were in. The trick was to right the plane and resume controlled flight as soon as possible. I'm not sure what we expected to learn from this exercise. It was crazy kid stuff really and had we been caught at it we would have been washed out and sent to the infantry in less time than you could say Jack Robinson. Fortunately no one ever knew about this but us. We did not talk out of school lest we be out by our own hand.

We also tested the limits of speed and performance at every opportunity. We learned to "push the envelope" to its ragged edge, flying lower, faster, farther—doing anything new and different. Who could possibly have more fun than a twenty-two-year-old farm boy loose in the world flying a Lightning? We pushed it hard and pushed it often. How great that was. I was ecstatic nearly every hour of the day.

Finally, with our required hours fulfilled, we were advised by the major, who commanded our squadron, that we could, if we wished, map out a program for the AT-17 and run a low-level course. This would mean flying nearly three hundred miles or more at fifty to seventy-five feet. We were to map out a course to fly and then execute it. As soon as the major made the offer my hand went up, and I said, "I want it."

San Joaquin Bill rides again. Another of the Gun Ho Crew then asked me, "How about if I go with you?"

"Fine with me," I said. "Let's go tomorrow."

This offer was music to a fighter pilot's ears. Low-level was the most exciting flying to be had and even in the old Bamboo Bomber it would be some kind of fun to undertake. Since we had been flying the Phoenix area at ten thousand feet for many days, we decided that we didn't really need to map out a complete course. We knew the area like the backs of our hands, or so we thought, and a few checkpoints would be enough to get us through. So we marked our maps with several separated points and made ready to run our routine. Somewhere along the line a short circuit had developed between our brains and our bodies, and we would soon discover it to our great regret.

Chapter Fifteen: Low Over Desert Sand—With Feathers

The next morning we picked up our AT-17 and commenced flying our low-level route. We headed out from Williams Field just before 9 a.m. and began to fly at seventy-five feet over the expansive desert that covered that area. I soon began to realize that my knowledge of the area gained from ten thousand feet was worth next to nothing. I could see my very-near surroundings and that was all. Soon I was watching my instruments and wishing I had made better plans. I began to regret the onset of laziness that put me in this situation.

My copilot and I knew that there was a very low range of hills east and south of Williams Field, which we could pick up easily. We would fly along its base, following this natural course until we would locate an iron mine that would serve as our first checkpoint. The mine was located near a break in the mountains. There we would fly through the break and out into the open desert.

We located the mountains quite easily since they were visible from a considerable distance. We swung around below the ridge top with the hills on our right wing as we moved further south at 50 feet, looking for the mine. The expected half-hour went by quite quickly with very little talk in the cockpit. The 50-foot altitude was a rather intense experience, and there was no time for idle chatter.

Soon we began seeing Indian teepees strung out along the base of the hills. I had never seen anything like this before, so I took the plane lower to get a closer look. Soon we were just above the teepee poles, roaring along at maybe twenty-five feet above ground. This generated prop-wash problems for the residents of the several narrowly separated villages we flew over. I could see chickens flying up the hillside, while dogs, goats, and people ran both directions, attempting to escape from the screaming motor-powered banshee that appeared from nowhere and raised a huge cloud of dust as it passed. What the Indians thought of us I could only guess, but I imagine the Great Spirit heard many loud calls for our destruction in those minutes that must have seemed like hours to them. What was fun for us was definitely not fun for them. We really raised hell with the place.

In the midst of all that excitement we somehow missed our checkpoint and wound up flying quite a ways before we were able to locate what we thought was our goal. There on the ridge was an iron mine like the one we were seeking. We latched onto this and soon found a low spot in the hills through which we flew on out into the desert just like we had planned. Unfortunately, I had been following the mountains rather than my instruments, and the course had taken a turn away from our original course. We exited the hills, flying in the wrong direction. Instead of flying back toward Phoenix we were actually headed more toward Tucson. Added to that we were running low on fuel. Just at that moment the unfamiliar sound of Morse code began to emanate from our earphones. Something unexpected was happening, and we were right in the middle of it.

My copilot opened our manual and determined that the Morse code was coming from Davis-Monthan Field near Tucson, which was deep in restricted airspace. We had to land soon so rather than risk running out of gas over the desert we put in a radio call for permission to land there. The brown stuff was going to meet the fan when we did, but there was really no choice. Crashes in the desert were completely out of the question. Tail-in-a-crack time was coming up, but what the hell.

We received permission to land and approached the field from the north. From our approach we could see B-24 Liberators lined up on either side of the runway for a least a half a mile. There were trucks dropping off crews in large numbers as we approached. The runway was at least 8,000 feet long, and I seemed to need all of it.

Frightened out of my mind, I made what was my worst landing since Hancock Field in front of all of those bomber jocks. I bounced maybe four times before I got my AT-17 under sufficient control to taxi behind the jeep sent out to direct us. We parked the plane as directed, cut down the engines and got out. Soon a major drove up in a jeep and asked us, " What are you men doing here?"

I got to reply. "We were on a low-level flight from Williams Field, Sir," I said. "We missed our checkpoint and found ourselves low on gas and closer to here than anywhere else." I somehow managed to leave out the poor Indians.

The major accepted this without comment and after ordering us to remain with our plane he arranged to have us refueled. In the meantime he phoned our commander at Williams Field and informed him of the presence of two prodigal sons in the midst of restricted territory and asked what he should do with us. Apparently our commander said to hold us there, and he would be down shortly.

He arrived very quickly flying an AT-6 Texan, which flew twice as fast as our Bamboo Bomber. He approached the base commander. They exchanged salutes and then shook hands like the old friends they likely were. Then our commander came over to us and repeated the original question. "What are you men doing here?"

He was both amazed and unhappy. Once again I offered my truncated summary of our presence, again neglecting to mention Indians. He seemed to accept this, and we moved to the next phase. "Do you think you can fly a straight line back to Williams?" our major asked me.

"Yes, sir," I answered quickly, happy to have something positive to say.

"Good," he said. "Go do it! When you get there check in your parachutes and report to me in my office."

The headman's axe was rising, and I could see my head bouncing on the ground.

Chapter Sixteen: The Nature of the Problem

We climbed back into our lonely-looking AT-17 and took off as quickly as I could manage to run down between the two lines of massive Liberators and lift off of that restricted and very scary field. I found the proper compass heading and set a course for Williams Field, pushing our Bamboo Bomber to its limits. I knew there was no way I could outrun the major's AT-6, but I wanted to get this over with as soon as I could. Then I noticed a slight movement to my right and turned to see what might be happening there. Our commandant was sitting just off of my right wing in breathlessly close formation. He was staring right at my right ear as if he wished to visually drill a hole in my mastoid process. He was so close I could actually see his eyes beneath his leather helmet. I waited for him to move out, but this did not happen. The major stayed right there all the way back to base, which did nothing to ease the nervous strain of that afternoon.

I told my copilot to watch the compass while I concentrated on altitude and speed. There would not be one foot of variation in altitude or one degree from true course. The tension was absolutely thick as we concentrated on our tasks. Both of us were so nervous that we were close to being physically sick to our stomachs in fear of what lay ahead. Our flying careers could very well be over within another hour, all because we got caught up in Indian feathers and scattering goats and dogs. I had never been so uptight in my life as I was on that flight.

Soon Williams Field appeared and I lined up for what could be my last air approach to anywhere. Only when I started down did the major move out to a greater distance and allow me room to safely land. Somehow, at that moment, I managed something I seldom had accomplished in an AT-17. I absolutely greased the landing, touching down with smooth precision just like I knew what I was doing.

There was relief for about two minutes or the time it took the two of us to deplane.

Once on the ground we proceeded to the equipment room to check in our chutes, which we were no longer going to need. Those who do not fly never hit the silk. It was an ominous moment. Once we had checked in our gear, we walked unsteadily to the major's office, literally shaking in our boots. Our swan song was rapidly approaching.

We found the appointed office and entered in proper military fashion. We came stiffly to attention like a couple of wooden soldiers and waited for the man to hand us our heads. The major looked at us almost quizzically as if searching for just the right words and said to us, "Gentlemen, I have little a problem, and I need you to help me with it. Report to me here in the morning at nine o'clock."

In a state of disbelief we mumbled, "Yes, sir," more or less at once, turned about-face and left the office. Two steps beyond the closed door, euphoria struck like a five-hundred-pound bomb. 'Gentlemen,' he had said. Cadets were always called Mister! Gentlemen meant we were graduates, real pilots. No more cadet time. There was, of course, a price to be paid but we two literally leaped off the ground and slapped hands high above our heads as we headed out of the building at the double quick.

The Dodgers claim to have invented the High Five, but my partner and I were experimenting with it thirty years ahead of them. The major was not going to wash us out after all. Oh, did we feel good!

The next morning we were in the major's office at 9 a.m. sharp. Our leader took us around behind the administration building where we found some digging going on between buildings, which stretched out for nearly 100 yards to another building. There was a mechanical trencher sitting at the head-end of a 15-inch deep by 12-inch wide ditch that would one day hold a buried water pipe. The major informed us that this was the only mechanical tool he could get and that it would not last nearly long enough to traverse the necessary distance. Since there were no spare parts with which to repair the thing when it inevitably did break, we were needed to lessen the burden of the machine, John Henry style.

My partner was issued a pick, and I was given a shovel. We were turned over to a crotchety corporal who was in charge of our detail. He was our boss. He loved every minute of the next three days as he carefully directed our digging efforts in the concrete-hard dirt in the one-hundred-degree-plus heat of early June. In a week he would have to salute us as officers, but in the meantime he owned our butts and made the best possible use of them.

At the end of the first three-hour session of digging in the flinty soil, both of us had developed massive and numerous blisters on our non-labor-hardened hands. We suffered in silence.

The next morning we were careful to show up with appropriate work gloves so that we might survive the morning. The second day was identical to the first with three hours of extremely hard labor resulting in a few measly feet of not-deep-enough trench which we had to go back and fix to be sure the thing was exactly 15 inches deep. Then I got to redo several feet of sidewall work to get to the exactly 12-

inch width. Our boss never once allowed less than perfection, and he lorded it over these two officer candidates as if he was Julius Caesar himself, though I suspected Caligula was more accurate.

Twice during that second morning frustration overtook me, and I flung down my shovel and said something like, "He can't do this to me!" and started to walk off the job. Each time I managed to get my Teutonic temper under control and force myself back to the task. I realized I was being severely tested, and I slowly hardened my resolve to soldier on through. "This too shall pass, Bill."

Once again, my mother's words advised me. "This too shall pass."

And so it did.

Chapter Seventeen: Graduation

Our graduation ceremony was scheduled for a Saturday afternoon. Several of us had family coming down for the event, and I had to pick up my group at the train station. I drove my Buick convertible to town to fetch my mother, my aunt, and my sister who had come down to see me complete my journey. Afterward they would drive my car home since I would be moving on soon and would not be able to take it with me.

The ceremony was to be held on a raised platform with a viewing stand to the west side. There the guests would have the afternoon sun at their backs and would be shielded from the early summer glare while watching the proceedings.

The graduates would ascend from ground-level seating to the platform and then proceed to a table where a sergeant sat. Our certificates, which ended our period of enlistment and another certificate granting us commissions as second lieutenants and pilots, were stacked neatly on the tabletop. When one of us mounted the stairs and appeared before the sergeant we were given first our termination of enlistment and then our appointment to commission. Standing next to the sergeant was the colonel, our base commander, who would shake our hand and congratulate us on completing requirements for graduation and welcome us to the society of commissioned officers.

My turn came in my usual place, near the front of the alphabetical line. When my name was called, I mounted the stairs happily and marched the five or so strides to the table where I was presented with my papers. At that moment I ceased using my old serial number, 39088402, which was retired, and I assumed a new number, 0748892, identifying me as a newly commissioned second lieutenant and pilot.

Then I turned to the colonel, came to attention, and saluted smartly. He returned my salute and then offered his hand to me, which I accepted. I had never met the man before and was quite taken by his command presence. He was well turned out in full dress uniform and stood several inches taller than me. He was an older man and a full bird colonel, with light-colored hair and very blue eyes. He had my full attention. I was pleased to be congratulated by such a man.

Bill Behrns (Bill Behrns' collection)

From there I marched across the stage, left to right, to where a second sergeant sat at another table where there was a stack of scrolls. These documents contained our next duty assignments. Next to that table stood the overall commander of air operations for our area, a brigadier general. I obtained my scroll from the general, whom I saluted and who then shook hands with me. At that point as a newly commissioned officer and gentleman (by act of Congress), I marched to where my sister stood waiting at the end of the platform. Smiling proudly she pinned my silver wings above the pocket on my coat and pinned my lieutenant's bars on my shoulders completing the right of passage.

I then advanced down the stairs down to ground level where other newly appointed officers were gathered. There we opened our scrolls and read the words that would change the directions of our careers thenceforth. My orders read "Proceed immediately to Muroc, California, (now Edwards Air Force Base) for instruction in gunnery and fighter tactics in P-38s." There it was in black and white. The dream of the undersized kid from French Camp was actually coming true.

Chapter Eighteen: Muroc

At the end of graduation ceremonies, the newly minted officers were summoned to a gathering in a large building a short distance away in which a spread of food and drink had been assembled. Attendees included supervisors, administrative officers, instructors, and new officers. No one else was allowed inside.

Inside we found ourselves some finger food and a mildly alcoholic drink and began to mix with the people who had trained us. In this environment regular military discipline was suspended, and things were pretty much in the open. We stood at ease amongst each other and talked for a while, more or less as equals. While a modicum of respect prevailed, it was pretty much an anything goes atmosphere. We were free to talk openly with our superior officers, and most of us did just that.

During these proceedings, my squadron commander came up to me and addressed me, using a term that surprised me, but set the tone for open and frank talk. "Behrns, you son of a #%*+#," he said. "I know you lied to me over that low-level incident, and I should have washed you out right there. I didn't because you had completed all of your training, and we had way too much invested in you. On top of that you were too good a pilot to throw away. Otherwise you would be gone."

I came back just as frank but a bit less aggressive. "You know," I said, "I thought that ditch-digging thing was a bit over the top. I'm a farm kid and I know something about digging, but that concrete dirt and the smart-assed corporal just about did me in. I know why you did it, and believe me I actually appreciate it. You wanted to get my attention, and you certainly did. I got some focus out of that, but I'm not sure I'd do that to anyone else."

The major smiled and offered me his hand. "You're too good to lose, Bill. Keep that focus." With that he turned and walked away. I still hadn't mentioned any teepees or Indians.

I was later told that this practice of mixing together as equals was discontinued with later classes. I'm not sure how I feel about that since I think I got something out of it. Apparently somebody complained to higher-ups, and the mixing stopped. I suppose all good things must come to an end, but it was good to clear the air that day.

The next morning, I was on the train to Muroc Field where training for combat was to begin. Muroc was south of us by 250 miles and located in California's high desert. The field was little more than a dry lakebed and early summer temperatures were described as literally hotter than Hades.

It has been said that 90 percent of success is just showing up, and at Muroc, that certainly proved to be the case. The heat was several clicks beyond scorching every day I was there, with temperatures often topping 120 degrees Fahrenheit. The big challenge each day was to climb into your Lightning, start the motors, and taxi the mile and a half to the takeoff area without overheating your engines, which would leave you stranded for half an hour waiting for your engine temperatures to drop below redline. The pilot in such a situation was awarded the honor of sitting in a broiling cockpit while his craft slowly cooled down. During such an ordeal one could easily develop sympathy for lobsters. Another way to beat the heat was to rev up and roar down to the end of entryway at one-hundred-plus miles per hour using your brakes to keep from lifting off. This worked unless you overheated your brakes, which could ruin both pads and rotors meaning you got to help the mechanics change those parts in all that desert heat before you could take off. I managed to avoid both kinds of overheating and proceeded routinely. I believe my off-the-books extra hours at Williams Field gave me an advantage over some of the less-experienced fliers in my group.

Aerial gunnery was composed of strafing targets made up of large stacks of hay bales onto which large circular targets were attached. We would approach these stationary targets at a 20- to 25-degree angle and begin firing at about 400 yards. We were generally flying at 250 to 300 miles per hour on approach, and we would walk our rounds up to and through the targets as we moved past. I tended to hold a little low to start with to avoid overshooting. If I started high, it was difficult to depress the nose to correct. Raising the nose was not a problem. Getting too low could result in an unscheduled belly landing you might not survive.

Our Lightnings were wonderful gun platforms since the pilot did not have to adjust for torque on approach. Counter-rotating propellers provided a level of stability unmatched in any other fighter plane. Added to that was the concentration of firepower available from the "suite" of weapons located in the nose of the plane, directly in front of the pilot. Other fighters had their guns mounted in the wings beyond the prop. These guns, usually six of them, fired at converging angles until the vectors merged together for the full effect. Beyond that point the pattern began to diverge again, curtailing efficiency. In a P-38 the props were mounted out beyond the guns, out of harm's way. When the pilot activated his electronic gun sight, he was staring right straight at the maximum point of his pattern. What he saw was what he got at any range.

Another interesting thing we Lightning pilots encountered was the rather exciting smell of burned cordite in the cockpit. No other fighter provided this sensory experience. Anyone who has ever smelled burned gunpowder knows that it gets you going.

We learned to fire our guns in short bursts for two important reasons. The first was to conserve ammunition for the trip home. Who knew whom you might meet out there. The second reason was to preserve our equipment. Too many rounds through a gun barrel without proper cooling could burn out the lands or warp the barrel. Either thing would ruin the accuracy of a fine weapon. Burnouts also caused maintenance problems. Bad guns had to be replaced and new ones boresighted for accuracy. This took considerable time, which could be avoided if the pilot simply paid attention to proper technique. Good strafing took discipline and control. Waste not, want not. Still, strafing could sometimes require bursts up to three seconds long due to the presence of targets strung out along the ground. One- or two-second bursts were better for the guns. A Lightning carried 500 rounds per gun of .50 caliber machine gun ammo and 168 rounds of 20 mm cannon.

Air-to-air shooting was an entirely different activity. Here short bursts, one after another, were often required to keep bullets on a dodging, weaving target. At Muroc we seldom got to shoot at those kinds targets since the variety of tow planes used to move our targets through the air were uniformly slower and less agile than enemy fighters were likely to be. Targets were towed straight and slow with plenty of room between banner and tow plane to allow us to get the hang of leading a target without shooting down a friendly.

As a country kid I had some bird-hunting experience and

understood the basics of leading a target in order to deliver shot to the flying dove or pheasant. A coach I knew compared the tactic to playing catch with a football. If you throw a pass to a running receiver you must throw the ball to where the runner will be when the ball arrives rather than to where he is at the moment of release. Without the "lead" the ball will fall far behind its intended target. The same principal applies to hot lead in search of an airplane. Many of our great aces during this war were first of all duck hunters.

We mastered the basics of gunnery rather quickly, and we were into fighter tactics after a couple of weeks. We were first taught how to fly in formation. We had a basic four-plane formation in the shape of a square "box." The flight leader was out front with a wingman on either side. The guy in back of the box was known as "tail-end Charlie." The man on the left side of the formation was the "element leader" of the basic two-plane formation in which American aviators fought. Charlie would follow left-element lead as his wingman when the formation broke into teams of two. The right-side plane stayed on the wing of the flight leader.

Larger formations of eight or twelve planes would position four-plane boxes into a larger box with four in front, four on each side, and four behind. Even larger groups positioned themselves in keeping with this same, organizing formula. Groups of up to forty-eight P-38s were often seen in Europe. In the Pacific, groups that large were rare. In Burma, the average flight was eight planes.

For a few sessions, we practiced holding formation and breaking into elements. We learned to maintain wingman position and how to re-form our larger formations. And then, quite suddenly, our training ended. There was a situation on the northern Oregon coast that demanded the presence of P-38s. I was abruptly and unexpectedly assigned there. I packed in a hurry and headed north by train for Olympia, Washington.

Chapter Nineteen: Patrolling the Northwest Coast

The sudden change of assignment was brought about by the appearance of a Japanese mini-submarine off the coast at Brookings, Oregon. The sub had apparently surfaced and launched balloons filled with leaflets announcing the coming invasion of the United States by the Japanese Empire. The leaflets contained instructions to the local population on how they should conduct themselves when the invasion force arrived if they wished to be well treated. Panic spread rapidly throughout the Northwest Territory in anticipation of the coming yellow peril. The United States government attempted to counter this reaction by assigning a squadron of P-38 pilots to be based at Olympia County Airport in Washington with responsibility for patrolling the coast from Puget Sound all the way south to Fort Bragg, California. A dozen P-38s with crews were assigned to handle this task.

As things worked out, the train I was on changed tracks from Southern Pacific to Western Pacific whose rails ran right across the back portion of our family ranch in French Camp. I hadn't been home in over a year and sat longingly at the window looking at my childhood home passing by, hoping to see one or more of my family out and about. I saw no one, and the poignant moment passed. I would not lay eyes on home again until late April of 1945, when I returned to the States from overseas duty.

I arrived at Olympia and took a taxi from the train station to the airport. As I arrived I could see a line of P-38s sitting along the runway. There were ground crew attending to them.

I carried my barracks bag with me to the main building

where I found a captain and a sergeant sitting at two small tables. Captain Arnold Laven had just come back from a yearlong combat tour in the Aleutian Islands of western Alaska where the Japanese had actually invaded United States territory. His assignment would be to assemble and prepare squadrons for overseas duty. Captain Laven was a jovial and gregarious person who quickly made friends. He would be promoted to major the following month. I found out from him that I was the first pilot to report, and he further informed me that our immediate mission would be to patrol a large area of the northern coast and nearby waters looking for submarines or invasion craft.

A few minutes later, a sergeant walked in carrying his barracks bag and announced that he was leaving for another duty station and asked if anyone would like to buy his car. With no hesitation, I put up my hand and said, "Yes." I inquired as to the make and model and found out he had a 1934 Dodge coupe, tan in color and in excellent shape. I paid him $150.00 for it on the spot. I would have that car for quite a long time as things progressed. When it came time for me to go to my next duty station, I called home, and my father and older sister came up to Olympia by train and drove the coupe home where it would await my return. It stayed in my family for seven full years. How little we know when we do things.

I soon found myself the only pilot in the group with his own car, and that made me very popular with rest of the guys who regularly rode with me to the nearby Olympia Brewing Company at Tumwater where the company provided free beer to servicemen.

The brewery really went all out to please our servicemen. We would drive out to the site and enter into a large indoor serving area where a huge four-sided bar was set up. There were four kegs of beer set up along the bar, and six serving girls were there to keep our steins constantly full. The guys could and did drink as much as they wanted, and somehow or another no one ever became unruly or uncontrollable while drinking there, at least not that I was ever aware of. Each evening soldiers from Fort Lewis flocked to join us, and the group consumed many gallons of what the brewery called "The Finest Product of the Brewer's Art." Nearly all of these personnel were destined for overseas duty and combat, and this was a tribute the locals could pay to all of them before they left. Our military put no restrictions on the place.

I was not a beer drinker, so I did not benefit from the free suds, but goodwill from the other flyers brought me other benefits along the way. The guys were only too happy to help out whenever I needed something, so it worked out well for everyone.

Our flying assignment was meant to alleviate the tense situation in the Northwest where people still expected the Japanese to arrive at almost any time. We went out nearly every day, flying north through the Strait of Juan de Fuca and out over Puget Sound, then south down the coast to Crescent City, California, where we turned inland and flew back to Olympia. The patrol took about two hours to complete depending on the weather, which was downright atrocious on many days. It rained almost constantly on the Olympic peninsula but usually cleared at least somewhat for our return following the Willamette Valley north.

There was a lot of coastal fog to contend with on takeoff that made it difficult to see the tall pine trees at the end of our runway, which we had to clear before starting our sweep. Oftentimes the soup was so thick that I lost sight of my wingman shortly after forming up. A flight was made up of four planes, and the situation was quite dangerous, especially for newly-minted pilots like we were.

We were fortunate to lose only one pilot during our time at Olympia. The pilot was Second Lieutenant Bingham, and he caused his own demise by trying to do something he thought would be fun. He spotted a fishing boat containing two anglers on a small lake in a mountainous area not far from our base. He decided to buzz this boat for the fun of it and dropped low over the water and made a high-speed pass on the fishermen, who were quite frightened by his presence at such close quarters. Bingham then turned back around and returned for another low-level run, and this time the fishermen were so scared that they jumped out of their boat rather than be crashed into by the big Lightning. As he pulled up and out of that second pass, Bingham turned the wrong way and flew straight into the side of a mountain at 250-plus miles per hour. He was probably looking back over his opposite shoulder at the anglers-turned-swimmers as he made his turn. I hope he died happy.

I remember that afternoon well as our Dodge ambulance returned from picking up the dead lieutenant. A stretcher carrying his remains was pulled from the vehicle with the body concealed under a full-length, white sheet. There were large patches of blood at several places on this cover. The body leaked blood on the ground as it was carried to the morgue inside the base hospital. It was a sobering experience for the rest of us, and no one ever tried anything like that again during this tour of duty. It was a tough lesson for young pilots, and I never forgot it.

We continued with this patrol assignment for nearly two months, using our Lightnings for the exact purpose for which they had been built. In 1937, looking forward to approaching war, the US Army Air Corps put out a contract for a long-range coastal interceptor that could be used to defend the country from naval and air attacks from the sea. Lockheed Aircraft Corporation of Burbank, California, responded to this request with a design from a young engineer named Clarence (Kelly) Johnson. On learning of the government's interest, Johnson began toying with designs, which first took form on a restaurant napkin. Johnson showed his half-dozen doodles to senior engineer Hall Hibbard, indicating a preference for a boxy twin-boom design with twin engines. Hibbard liked the thinking Johnson presented to him and gave the young genius permission to proceed with a more complete design.

Just under one year later, the XP-38 was trucked out to Muroc Field for its initial test flight. The end result of the program gave pilots like me a flexible, long-range aircraft, well suited for patrol duties like the ones I was now flying. The Atlanta, as it was first called, was renamed Lightning by the British in 1940, and the name stuck. The plane was not initially seen as a mainline fighter, but its ability to fly long distances immediately thrust it forward into that endeavor. As time passed, it became plain that the P-38 was an enormously effective fighter along with the amazing number of other things this plane could do. Lightnings scored the first American victories of the war against both the Japanese and the Germans and went on to destroy more enemy aircraft than any other Allied plane. Nearly every fighter plane record was set in a P-38. It was beginning to become apparent that my preferred airplane was the right one to be flying.

Chapter Twenty: Miami and Points East

Our time at Olympia ended. We were put on a train and shipped to Miami, Florida. Due to the fact that my name started with a letter near the beginning of the alphabet, I was given the assignment of counting noses and keeping track of my squadron mates until we arrived at our destination. At Miami we were checked into the Fountainblue Hotel, which was the ritziest address in town. I immediately went out and rented a convertible from a large lot just across the street from the train station. Several of the other pilots did the same thing. We were in Miami Beach for ten days and all of us planned on enjoying ourselves. My duty was to report to military headquarters twice a day waiting for new orders. The orders finally came, and my next job was to locate everyone and have them ready for departure from the bus station for a ride to the airport by 6 a.m. the next morning.

At the airport I was given a sealed envelope, by an officer, to be opened 30 minutes after takeoff. This would reveal our destination without allowing anyone on the ground prior knowledge of our assignment. Thirty minutes into the flight I opened the envelope and read its contents. Then, passing the notice to another pilot, I loudly spoke one word, "BURMA!" We were headed for the China, Burma, India Theater of war—the dreaded CBI.

We were flying in a B-24 bomber converted into a cargo plane. The plane had no passenger seats, and there was a wooden floor upon which we placed our barracks bags. We used those bags as pillows whenever we tried to sleep. There were no windows to speak of and it was very dark inside for our entire journey. It was also incredibly noisy with no insulation on the walls and very cold for the same reason. This was not a comfortable way to fly, but it got the job done. We would emerge from this monocoque-fuselage nightmare feeling like Jonah coughed up on the beach.

Our route took us from Miami Beach south to Georgetown, British Guiana, where we spent the night. The next morning we flew east to the Ascension Islands, a tiny strip of land in the Atlantic, where we refueled and set off for the Ivory Coast of Africa, landing at Accra. From there our converted B-24 cargo plane took us across Africa to Aden where we refueled again and changed planes to a luxury DC-3 passenger plane with padded seats and windows by each seat. We then set off in solid comfort for Karachi, Pakistan. In route to this stop, we crossed the Arabian Sea where we encountered a German U-boat sitting on the surface. Our pilot directed our attention to its presence, and then turned to get a closer look. The Kraut apparently took this as the beginning of an attack and fired at us with his deck gun. The first round passed harmlessly behind us, but the second dry-burst was very close to our left wing. Our pilot decided he had seen enough, banked away to the right, and departed the danger zone. A shot on target would have wiped out thirty-four pilots at once: our thirty-two from the 459th and two more flying the DC-3. The outcome in an entire theater of war might have been changed right then and there.

We arrived at Karachi unscathed and stayed there for several days. We were lodged in a nice hotel. Two of our officers had a room on the ground floor. One of them went out while the other was taking a shower. A window had been left open to cool the room. A native entered through that window and stole the wallet out of the pilot's pants. He was exiting the room via the window when the officer emerged from the bathroom and saw the man trying to flee. The pilot went to the window and shouted the universal call of "stop thief," and sure enough a policeman stepped around the corner and nabbed the culprit on the spot. The purloined wallet was returned, and then things got interesting. The policeman chained the thief to a nearby lamppost, and there he would stay for nearly two days. As people passed the man they threw rocks at him, cursed him, spit on him, beat him with canes, and generally made life miserable for the offender. At the end of the first day, a policeman brought a bowl of rice to the criminal, which he dumped on the walk in front of the man. The captive immediately dropped to his knees and began to scoop up the meal with his fingers, dirt and all. He was left there overnight without additional clothing and reviled again the next morning. Near the end of the second day, one of our pilots went out and found a policeman and asked him to release this man since he had suffered enough and had not gotten the wallet in any event. The pilot was told that the man was not being punished because he stole, but rather because he was caught. Theft, it seems, was condoned while apprehension was not. Interesting place, Pakistan. This was our first insight into Indian justice.

From Karachi, we moved on to Calcutta and there we were lodged in the Grand Hotel. After a week, we moved on to Dacca in the nation of India. There we were to take delivery of a dozen thoroughly-used P-38s that had seen a year's combat in North Africa. These planes were shot up and used up, but they were at least ours. It was now October of 1943, and the 459th Squadron was about to enter the war.

Chapter Twenty-One: Calcutta

We were at the magnificent Grand Hotel for about a week. It was a well-established site with excellent fixtures and numerous ceiling fans throughout the building, which made do for air conditioning of a sort. Compared to buildings around it, the Grand was cool and comfortable, definitely a cut above. One nice feature on the ground floor was an expansive lounge area furnished with comfortable, overstuffed furniture in Victorian English fashion where guests and occupants could gather to socialize. Being new to the premises, I had yet to have a guest to entertain, but that would soon change. For the moment, I was just an American flyer with no airplane and subsequently bored out of my mind.

There was a large, covered market nearby. The building must have enclosed at least three acres and was open at the sides so that the breeze could pass through but well-roofed against the heavy monsoon rains that occurred seasonally each year. One reason I wanted to go there was to find out what time it was in Calcutta since I had flown clear across the entire country with no way to check on time. The sun was telling me nine o'clock while my watch was arguing for 6:30. Included in this vast marketplace were individual vendor stalls of nearly every type featuring, clothing, jewelry, foodstuffs, trinkets, tools, and just about anything else a man or woman could want. Somewhere in this labyrinth there had to be a watch vendor who could get me straight with the correct time. Boldly, I set out in search of such a person or place.

While I was on my quest to obtain the desired information,

I happened upon a booth where a jeweler had a large selection of watches including American and European brands. There was a young woman standing a few feet away who was eyeing some jewelry. She was without a doubt the loveliest person I had ever seen anywhere. The kid from French Camp couldn't help but stare. How long I looked at her I really don't remember since time is of little import at such moments, but eventually she noticed the young man in uniform looking her way. Our eyes met. She smiled at me in an open and gentle way, which made me feel welcome in her presence. I closed the gap between us by speaking across the corner of the counter where we stood on opposite sides, and announced myself with a simple "Hello." I went on to ask her what time it was in Calcutta, hoping she would understand me. When she answered me in absolutely flawless British, I was utterly enthralled.

We got to talking, and she told me her grandfather had been minister of rice distribution for the British Government in Northern India, and as a result of strong government connections she had been schooled in England and had graduated from Oxford University where she met and later married a major in the British Army. The Japanese had killed her new husband in the first year of the war, leaving her with a three-year-old son. It was a common-enough story in the India of that time.

This brought the conversation around to me. I told her I was just in from America and didn't know my way around anything and would really like to know what a person could drink to cool off in this very hot, humid country. She told me iced coffee was best, so I invited her to join me for one and she accepted. We found a vendor who could fill our need, and we sat and talked for a while, cooling off and becoming friends. We got along splendidly, rapidly becoming easy in each other's company. As our time ended, she told me her name was Paula. When I asked if I could see her again, she gave me a phone number where she could be reached, which I gratefully accepted. We parted casually, she going her way and me going mine. I now had an interest in this city beyond the time of day.

The following morning, I called the number Paula had provided, and when she came to the phone, I invited her to join me for dinner that evening at the Grand Hotel. I must say I was very pleased when she accepted my invitation.

We met at the Hotel early the next evening for supper. It was a casual affair, and we enjoyed the good food and our time together. Neither of us drank much alcohol, preferring Coca Cola, which was enormously popular in India. The hotel had a very good dance band that played during dinner and later into the evening, specializing in American Big Band music of the 1930s and 40s. Although not much of a dancer, I braved the dance floor a couple of times because I couldn't stand not to. Paula danced beautifully while I moved around a little and watched a lot. The lady stood about five feet, six inches and had a spectacular figure. Her hair was coal black and hung to just below her shoulders, framing a classic face with straight patrician features and a clear complexion, which was just slightly medium, speaking softly of her eastern heritage. She seemed to flow across the dance floor with an almost feline grace as if she was actually suspended a few millimeters above the surface rather than attached to it. As someone who had studied and played music, I appreciated her ability to blend the ethereal and physical so sublimely. It was difficult not to simply stand and stare. I managed it through conversation, and the evening passed quite well. We made a date for later in the week before parting for the night.

Paula and I spent time together each day while I remained in Calcutta, and we became good friends. I was to spend time with this lovely, aristocratic young woman each time I came back to the city during my tour of duty. I would look her up, and we would go out for dinner and dancing. We were always platonic, just good friends, but it was exciting to be with her because everywhere she went, people noticed her and therefore paid attention to the both of us. She dressed in up-to-date western fashions, typical of London or Paris, and I was to discover that she had two servants, a man and a woman, dedicated to her comfort. Whenever I called her home, the man always answered and summoned her to the phone. There was a certain British ritual about it all.

Paula had a first-rate mind to compliment her beauty, and it was always a pleasure to be with her. On several occasions, my squadron mates told me I had found a real peach of a girl at which I just smiled and went on my way. I didn't talk to them about Paula as I have always felt a man should not talk about what he does with other people, as it is not fair to them to so do. I have always held to that rule, and it has served me well.

There were many other things to see in Calcutta. With little else to do besides wander, I took in as many sites as I could and was constantly amazed by the things I saw. Large numbers of homeless and indigent people crowded the sidewalks at all hours of the day, many of them lying asleep in the midst of everything so that walking a straight line to anywhere was just about impossible. I found out that most of these were without homes to go to and many of these were also without jobs. They lived from hand-to-mouth and did their best to survive right where they were. For most, there was simply nowhere else to go. If someone was lucky, they might live underneath a bridge or other raised platform that provided at least some shelter but most were right out in the open, rain or shine. It was livable for about two-thirds of the year but during the constant torrential rains of the monsoon season many hundreds died of exposure and hypothermia. Children and the aged were particularly at risk. The rigid caste system added to the misery. For those in the lower strata of society, India was a tough place to live.

Another thing that surprised me was the freedom of animals within the city, particularly of cattle that roamed at will absolutely everywhere. Cattle were sacred to Hindus, and it was forbidden to interfere with them in any way. The huge beasts roamed freely down the isles of the open market, knocking things down and grazing at will from the vegetable vendors displays. People backed away from them, stepped around them, and avoided touching them. They left piles of biochemical byproduct wherever it suited them, and at times they would lie down in the middle of sidewalk or street, stopping traffic completely until they felt like moving to somewhere else. No one disputed the cows' right to do this. It was just part of landscape of life in the city.

Monkeys could also be problematical if you weren't on your guard. They were numerous and vociferous in nearly every tree and would hurl fruit, nuts, and sometimes less mentionable objects down on the unsuspecting. We were not allowed to retaliate and gave them a wide birth whenever possible.

Sanitation under these conditions was somewhere between enormously difficult and totally impossible. There were not sufficient facilities for the huge indigent population, and they did their "duty" right where they were, a big share of the time leaving their mess to be lived in by everyone else. I was flabbergasted the first time I saw a woman, uh, "rain" on the public street by putting one foot down on the street and the other up on the sidewalk, lifting her skirt and half squatting as she "rained" in the gutter.

Men had an easier time since they simply hung themselves out there and drained their bladders regardless of where they were or who might be watching. I once saw a man walk up to a faucet on the street, drop all of his clothes—yep, all of them—and proceed to give himself a hand-done, very-public shower, as people walked by on both sides of him. He paid no heed to anyone, finished his job, dressed again, and walked away as if it was the most natural thing in the world, which to him it probably was. *Hey Bill, I don't think we're in French Camp anymore.*

The meat markets were fascinating. Halves and quarters of beef, pork, mutton, and lamb and assorted birds hung from poles strung horizontally above the ground, giving the would-be purchaser an eye-level experience with the vendor's wares—whatever they might be. The buyer had to judge his purchase through a solid layer of flies coating the swinging meat that was totally unprotected from insects or the elements as it was displayed. To better determine quality, the potential buyer would slap the side of beef or leg of lamb or whatever else with his open hand causing a loud noise and also causing the meat to suddenly move. This flushed the resident flies briefly into the air leaving the buyer with an unobstructed view of his potential purchase for a precious few seconds. Then the buyer and seller would begin the bargaining process, which could even involve another slap of the meat while the buyer tried to convince the seller his price was excessive. Soon a deal would be struck, rupees would change hands, and the buyer would move, purchase in hand or in the hand of a servant, down to another booth to purchase vegetables or condiments or whatever else might be needed for the next series of meals. Sanitation seemed to be a non-issue. The aromas that Mark Twain once described as "the strange and exotic odors of the orient" wafted through the air, mixed with odors of human and animal waste, unwashed bodies, and a variety of smells from rotting vegetation and raw sewage; the concoction left me with an olfactory memory I was to carry with me for more than half a century.

Traffic was always problematical even on the best of days. A major intersection of streets would be dominated by a raised wooden platform that stood a couple of feet taller than the street from which a traffic policeman, dressed in a resplendently ornate and colorful uniform, stood and directed traffic. These policemen stood out from the crowd like sunrise against darkness with their cone-shaped red hats; wide, gold shoulder boards; braided arms; and medaled chests. They stood on their raised "boxes" and moved mechanically through their routines, blowing whistles and waving traffic onward, left, right, stop, and ahead, with gestures straight out of Alphonse and Gaston of the Keystone Cops. The more remarkable fact was that neither drivers nor pedestrians seemed to pay one bit of attention to them.

In the midst of all of this was a monumental traffic jam caused by a bull and four cows that had lain down in one-half of the intersection, jamming all north and eastbound traffic, which precluded the normal movement of south and westbound traffic. Horns honking, manual horns with rubber ball-squeeze honkers, brakes screeching, engines roaring, people shouting, cops gesturing and whistling, and nothing, including cows, moving. It was almost like New York at rush hour. I was on foot and glad of it.

Another surprising thing I saw in the street was a lone man pushing a wheelbarrow in which there was nothing except his own scrotum, which filled the cargo area completely. He was obviously suffering from a disease called elephantiasis that causes extremity body parts to swell to enormous proportions while generating skin surfaces resembling elephant hide. I had heard of this disorder before but had never seen a living being trying to cope with it. The disease is caused by a filarial infection of threadlike round worms that destroy many of the lymph glands in an arm, foot, ankle, etc., and sometimes in the scrotum. The worms cause fluid to gather in the infected areas and the resulting swollen deformities are far beyond gross to look at. Like so many things in India the people made no attempt to conceal the offensive sight, choosing instead to deal with the condition openly as if it were perfectly normal to carry around testicles larger than two full-sized suitcases. There is an old army saying that an unusually brave and aggressive soldier has a bucket full of balls, but this fellow was close to needing a dump truck.

Anything I failed to understand about the things I observed, I took up with Paula at our next meeting, and she would patiently explain to California Bill what was actually going on from the point of view of a Calcutta resident. By the time I was ready to leave, I think I understood about half of it or at least some of it. One thing for sure was that Paula and I never ran out of things about which to talk.

When our squadron's time in Calcutta ended, we were transported farther north to Dacca in a C-47. Dacca sits inside Pakistan, between India and Burma. We were based at Kurmitola, just a few miles out of town. It was here we were given a squadron name and a number under which we would serve for the duration of the war. A small but storied group was being formed in upper-Assam. Two hundred or so support personnel arrived by sea, and thirty-two pilots came in by air. The Twin Dragon was stirring in its egg.

BOOK THREE: Into the Fight

Into the Fight (courtesy 459th Fighter Squadron)

Chapter Twenty-Two: The Reality of Things Military

So here it was, at the end of all that time and training. After seven months of basic flying, our field of one hundred had been reduced to a group of five. Five more weeks learning combat flying had washed out another 50 percent so that two or perhaps three of us remained to fly actual combat. Accidents would claim another one or more of those. I had made it to the war zone and would soon be assigned a P-38 in what proved to be the toughest aerial combat environment of the war. The next time I took to the air, the crazy Behrns kid from French Camp was likely to be hip deep in WWII action. I was one of a hundred — a modern Centurion. Who would have guessed?

As our unit began to gather at Olympia, we started to notice something about the composition of our group that set us to thinking some rather unkind thoughts. As pilots continued to arrive, it became obvious to us that no two of us came from the same state. When finally assembled, there were thirty-two pilots from thirty-two different states. Someone was trying to tell us something we really didn't want to hear. We had been very carefully selected to be the group no one noticed. Many units were chosen from within states or in some cases from fairly small localities. We were as opposite as we could possibly be from outfits of this kind. There was no local or regional cohesion to be found in our group. We were as singular as we could be. It was not really clear to any of us why we were so geographically fragmented until our assignment was given to us midway in our route to the orient.

As constituted, we were practically invisible to the public

eye, and there was a concerted effort made to keep us that way. This became more evident when six of the original pilots from the Olympia group were transferred out to make room for six officers of higher rank and longer service who would be our squadron leaders. They also were from individual states. A pattern was becoming clear.

It was becoming evident to all of us that this was not a chance occurrence. We had been very carefully selected so that the loss of any one of us we would be little noticed in the larger scheme of things. One lost pilot from any single state would cause no great concern when the Army Air Corps regularly lost dozens, if not hundreds, in any single day. What congressman or senator would loudly complain at the loss of a single pilot against that kind of background? Who would even notice?

We soon came to the conclusion that our unit was considered expendable and subsequent events did nothing to alter this perception in our minds. It was not a comfortable thought, but there it was. Replacements proved to be scarce; new planes were few and far between, and even spare parts were very hard to come by. We were in a backwater of the war and, communications were less than optimal. We made do as best we could. All of this was, as yet, in front of us as we made ready to board our C-47 and fly into the war zone. We would become the 459th Fighter Squadron upon landing at our new base near Dacca. We were at long last becoming a recognized unit.

Chapter Twenty-Three: The Twin Dragons Are Born

The 459th Fighter Squadron was first activated on September 1, 1943, as the fourth squadron in the 80th Fighter Group (SE), 311th Fighter Bomber Group. This actually happened in Upper Assam, making the 459th the third "Black Sheep" group of the war, meaning the group was formed entirely outside of the continental United States.

A normal fighter group is composed of three squadrons, so it was not surprising that the 459th was separated from the 80th Group to operate on its own. While the ground personnel came mostly from the 311th Group, the pilots came mostly from our unassigned group of P-38 coastal patrollers from Olympia, Washington. We were eventually brought together to form a unit at Kurmitola outside of Dacca, in the northernmost part of the China Burma India Theater. We were a long way from anywhere, a boondocks outfit if ever there was one. When we arrived in October, the outfit had no superior officers, no airplanes, and no nickname. A lot of things needed to happen before we could begin to think and act like a squadron.

The Twin Dragon idea seems to have originated with 1st Lieutenant Albert Curtis of Steubenville, Ohio, who began playing with drawings of a serpent body splitting off into two independent heads, emblematic of the twin-engine planes the group was going to fly. The original doodle contained a lightning bolt and a wing and gondola section resembling that found on a P-38. The first sketch apparently became enmeshed in a large map which traveled to Kurmitola when the rest of the group assembled and resurfaced there to be seen, discussed, and copied and, perhaps, improved by various crews until the image and idea were adopted by the group, appearing on shirts and jackets. Designs for the plane nose and body art soon followed, and the Twin Dragons were adopted by unanimous consent without a formal vote ever being taken.

After several months, in late March of 1944, Captain Leuhring, then our squadron commander, asked everyone for their written choice of names for our squadron, and Twin Dragons won out overwhelmingly. After that, letters, dispatches, and other documents generated by our unit carried that name. Our planes soon wore long green and white serpents from nacelle to tail on both sides of our Lightnings. Our mascot was a good one. We liked our Twin Dragon and saw to it that he was well fed.

Chapter Twenty-Four: Getting Organized

We flew into the battle zone, which was perhaps two hours from wheels up to touchdown at our base at Kurmitola, a few miles outside of the city of Dacca. We were now in an area where the Japanese Army Air Force (Rentai) was very active. Fortunately, we did not encounter any of them on our way in. We arrived in good order and deplaned not really knowing what to expect next.

One Captain James Ward was sent to receive us and met us at the orderly room to get us settled. The captain inquired as to who was in charge. While no one really was, I did have the alphabetical list in my hand, and I was suddenly front and center. I presented that to him and explained it had been my job to count heads at each stop on our way out here. He seemed to take that as a supervisory position and elevated me in his thinking to a position of some importance. "Behrns," he said to me, "put your bags over there in my tent."

I did so and, just like that, I had a roommate with rank. For the short time Ward was with us, just about two weeks, we became friends.

For the first few days we had no airplanes and, for all practical purposes, no commanding officer. We were soon assigned a commander named Captain John Fouts, who was attached to General Davidson's Tenth Air Force Command in Calcutta. Fouts, a holder of the Air Medal, had been in theater for thirty-four months and was about to be sent home in normal rotation, so he never really took control of our unit. Soon after being promoted to major, Fouts got caught up in some rotten weather and, after making several attempts to find a landing field, ran out of fuel and bellied in one of our P-38s. He survived the crash with little personal damage other than to his dignity. Fouts eventually went stateside and was replaced by Captain Verl Leuhring, who hailed from Leavenworth, Kansas. Five more superior officers were soon sent our way, and six of our original P-38 drivers were transferred out to make room for them. I understood later that a couple of those guys wound up in F-5 recon Lightnings out of Calcutta while the rest found their way into B-25 medium bombers. I could be mistaken about that, since nothing official ever came our way as to the disposition of our former squadron mates.

About three weeks after our arrival at Kurmitola, we began to get airplanes. A few well-used P-38s arrived, shipped to us by ferry pilots from battlefields in North Africa. These Lightnings were G and H models with few of the refinements Lockheed built into later planes. The planes had been "rode hard and put away wet," as an American cowboy would say it, but they were in flyable condition and a whole lot better than the nothing we had previously.

Under the skillful supervision of Lockheed Aircraft's Technical Representative, a graduate aeronautical engineer named Wayne Sneddon, the tired planes were quickly whipped into shape. Lockheed Tech Rep Bill Aycock was also involved in the restoration process. Shortly, we had combat-ready aircraft.

In the midst of this time period, it became the responsibility of the already-trained P-38 pilots to transition our new leaders into twin-engine flight. None of our superior officers had ever flown a P-38 before, most having spent their combat time in P-40s with one P-39 driver mixed in. I spent half a day training Captain Ward on the P-38 before he left us for his new assignment as aide to General Davidson in Calcutta.

With an experienced pilot as a student, the main task was to learn to handle two of everything at once. I sat on the edge of Captain Ward's cockpit and led him through the bits and pieces until we both felt he was ready to fly. He then took off in his Lightning, and I followed in another so that I could talk him through any questions he might have. The lessons went pretty well, and the skipper got up and down safely. I could still hear Mr. Caradies's voice echoing from Hancock Field, telling me that first you had to get airborne and then land safely. All else would be learned later. So here we were back at the beginning in a strange and distant land except that this time, I was the teacher rather than the student. The more things change the more they remain the same.

Others made the move to twin-engine flight without incident. This spoke of the overall skill those pilots possessed because many pilots were lost in making this transition, particularly from the P-39 to the P-38. One number seemed to make a whole lot of difference. Fortunately we lost no one in making the necessary adjustments.

Ferry pilots brought us more planes over the next couple of weeks. Before long we had a dozen well-used fighters with some new ones on the way, if and when they were to arrive. Captain Leuhring, now our commanding officer due to the departure of Major Ward, gathered our little group together and began the process of assigning airplanes to individual pilots. The first batch was numbered from 100 to 115 with no number 113 in the bunch. Naturally the gadfly from California had to ask where it was. "No one wants number 113," Captain Leuhring told me. "Unlucky," he added.

"I want it," I said, and I actually got it. I have always believed the best way to defeat superstition was to go straight at it, and that is what I did.

I never assigned a name to this airplane while I flew her. She was number 113, a P-38H with lots of experience. Somehow I failed to develop a fondness for this veteran of the North African War. She was a good, reliable flier, and I scored some minor victories with her, but no good name for her came to mind during the entire time we served together. Most of our time together was spent on routine patrol missions, although I did fly my first real combat mission in that airplane.

We did a lot of routine flying the first six weeks at Kurmitola. Some of it was regular training flights and some was escort duty with B-25 Mitchell bombers with which we rendezvoused as they came in from bases in India. In those early weeks we encountered no enemy fighters, although we knew there were over five hundred of them in our area of responsibility. This training time was good for us. We got used to the weather and the dense jungle surroundings and generally got in shape for what would soon be coming our way.

Chapter Twenty-Five: Into Combat

November of 1943 saw the Twin Dragons in the air, continuing patrol duty and escort flights usually over B-25 Mitchell Bombers classified as "mediums." Later on, we would spend more time with the "heavy" B-24 bombers on longer and more difficult missions. Most of these early missions were pretty much routine for the Lightnings. We did not encounter aerial resistance. A few weeks later, on December 26, 1943, things got a lot more interesting.

On the morning of December 26, we moved to the mess tent just before dawn and then assembled on the porch of the operations dacha and waited for orders we hoped would soon come. This day we were summoned to an intelligence briefing and given specifics for an attack on Anisakan Air Drome near Maymo. This was Japanese headquarters for their Central Burma operations. It was a very important target, and there was likely to be some serious resistance from the enemy.

Feelings ran high as we headed out to our fighters. The

P-38 E (Bill Behrns' collection)

Twin Dragon Squadron was going to draw enemy blood this day, and we could scarcely wait to get at them. The weather was clear and mild, as this was summertime in our half of the world. We got airborne early and formed up into traveling formations of four-plane boxes and began the nearly three-hundred-mile trek to our target. We moved quickly toward the Japanese airfield, encountering no resistance as we approached our objective, 295 miles from our base. We shook ourselves into a line and headed down for a strafing run.

I was third in line, as I remember it, and was aware that we had achieved at least some element of surprise, as there were several, perhaps a dozen, enemy aircraft parked in various revetments around the field. I found a likely target and hosed it with 50 calibers, then quickly found a lone truck to shoot up before passing out of the area.

As I climbed out of my dive, I found myself facing eight Japanese planes that had been lurking out of sight, waiting for us to come into their firing zones. They appeared to be Hamps, and I lined up on one of them as my guns came to bear and gave him a one-second burst, scoring several hits. The Hamp flew onward, losing altitude but still under control. He was going down, but I couldn't wait to see it. I was credited with a "probable" at the end of the mission. Everyone got back without damage, which meant that the Japs had not anticipated our presence in the area or there would have been heavy return fire. Now they knew we were here, and the next time would not be so easy.

Post-mission assessment credited our squadron with four planes destroyed and three damaged on the ground. Four others were attracted with no observable damage. It was exactly one year to the day that I had soloed at Hancock Field in Santa Maria, California.

Bill diving on target "Dragon Style" (Bill Behrns' collection)

Our guys were elated on the return trip to Kurmitola. We had suffered no losses, scored ground victories and one probable air-to-air win. The adrenalin was bleeding off, and our pilots were giddy over this first combat success. Some did wingovers and full rolls, while others sang upbeat songs into their radios. "When Johnny comes marching home again, hurrah, hurrah! We'll give him a hearty welcome then hurrah, hurrah!" Some of us joined in, some hummed along, and all of us enjoyed the moment. We were warriors! We had just had our first look at the Elephant!

Chapter Twenty-Six: Living At Kurmitola

Living conditions at Kurmitola were quite tolerable with the pilots being housed together as officers while the enlisted men and their crews had separate barracks of their own. We were housed in tents to begin with, while the operations areas were housed in more permanent buildings. The weather remained mild during our stay, and we were generally comfortable. As the days passed, bamboo shelters were constructed using native ingenuity and available materials, and we soon had suitable habitats for all who needed them.

The construction of these structures, I'm not quite comfortable calling them buildings, was simple and very straightforward, with three sides closed and often one side, away from prevailing winds, open to the weather. The big thing about the structures was that they did not leak. Temperature was seldom an insurmountable problem, but getting wet definitely could have caused big trouble. The native culture had long ago developed weaving techniques so that roofs of bamboo thatch were watertight. Snakes took up residence in the ceilings, but they subsisted on mice and insects and generally did not bother us. Tree snakes, on the other hand, were to be avoided at all costs since their preferred method of hunting was to drop on a victim from the limbs above, and their bite was almost instantly fatal.

One day several of us were gathered just off the flight line talking among ourselves when we heard a loud scream from out in one of the fields nearby. We ran toward the sound, and when we got there, we found a worker lying on the ground surrounded by his fellows. He was quite dead, and his companions explained that the worker had been bitten by a tree snake. One of my friends told me, "Bill, if one of those things ever bites you, just lie down."

"Why would I do that?" I asked in all innocence.

"Because you're already dead. You might as well go easy," he answered.

King Cobras were another matter altogether. They made their stealthy way into camp quite often, and we were always on the lookout for them. They were dangerous for several reasons but more so to the Indian workers than to the Anglo visitors because of the differences in dress that existed between us. Our workers tended to wear less clothing, particularly from the waist up than did any of us. This made them more vulnerable to cobra bites than we were since the King Cobra has very short fangs, and even a lightweight G.I. shirt might deflect a bite high on the torso, whereas the bare-skinned Indian would have no defense.

Unlike vipers and most other poisonous reptiles, cobras do not strike from a coiled position. They raise their heads nearly half their length above the ground and then lunge forward to strike their intended victim. If you see one a few feet away it is not difficult to avoid them. A practiced individual can even dodge a cobra strike if he sees it coming. Cobras are not fast moving. This is the fact that allows a mongoose to make his living. But, a man naked to the waist and walking through high grass can suddenly find himself looking a 12-foot King Cobra right smack in the eye. Such a person will likely not survive the next ten minutes. There were other, smaller cobras to deal with, and we developed habits to handle them as well. These intruders were two or three feet long and nowhere near as impressive as the Kings. They could, however, get into places where the bigger Kings were not likely to be found. We learned to check our beds at night to be certain we had no slithery guests, and we were instructed to wear our shoes to bed at night or to check them carefully in the morning to make certain they were not containers for snakes. Fortunately, our native workers knew how to handle such intruders, and we left to them the task of eliminating the poisonous pests. While it must be said that we lived with cobras, at least we did not die by them.

Food was another area that needs some commentary since soldiers in the field often complained about their mess situations in makeshift places carved out of the boondocks as our present base certainly was. Generally speaking the food was very good where we were, with typical meals being balanced and tasty. We had a professional butcher in the group who understood the needs of the squadron. He purchased cattle locally and cut them up for fresh meat every day. We had locally-raised poultry and eggs, plus a local form of butter for fresh baked bread. The butter was Indian style and had a slightly cheesy flavor to it, which I think the locals added as a kind of preservative to stretch out the useable life of the product. We also had fruit and potatoes bought from local farmers who were finding certain things about this war to their liking, since it brought them three hundred or so new customers, all of whom had money to spend and nowhere else to spend it.

Another feature of base life was that we held religious services on Sunday mornings. While I cannot recall our pastor's rank or name, I did attend regularly and enjoyed the devotion. We had services for Protestant, Catholic, and Jewish servicemen. These services were important to us. One should keep in mind that there are few, if any, atheists in a combat zone. There were times when we felt we could use a higher help, and most of us were not shy about asking for it.

One more personal experience should be shared at this point. I have been somewhat reluctant to write about this, but I have decided to share it as it illustrates things about life in this part of the world that cannot be otherwise explained, and if this book is to be true to life, the following story must be included.

One day Lieutenant Burdett Goodrich and I decided to travel into the city of Dacca for a sightseeing tour. We decided to travel by rickshaw rather than taking a truck as we felt we would see more and get a better feel for the place if we did not have to contend with the dense traffic ourselves. Our driver would take care of that for us.

Rickshaws were common all over the Far East. They were a takeoff on the British one-horse Hansom, although of much lighter and cheaper construction. The rickshaw was a two-wheel device pulled by a single man. Horses were scarce and expensive and few native cab drivers could afford them, so the men pulled the vehicles themselves on foot. A good "driver" could at least double the foot speed of a person walking and could cover many miles without stopping, slowing once in a while to catch a breath but always moving. A man could make a good living in the rickshaw trade, and many were available for hire in every city.

Once we had arrived at the outskirts of Dacca we found a stand area where a dozen or so rickshaw drivers were competing for attention. "Rickshaw, Sab," (short for Sahib). "Rickshaw today?"

We selected one and climbed aboard. The puller began to go forward. After a short ride, we spotted a native street-side fruit stand where we asked our driver to stop while Goodrich and I purchased one banana each as a snack for later. Mine turned out to be a little soft and not as tasty as I had hoped it would be. Disappointed, I tossed the remainder into the nearby gutter where it landed in the muddy, debris-filled water that was running through it. Instantly a figure appeared from the crowd of walkers and jumped into the gutter after that banana. It was a young man maybe 12 or 13 years old. He was skin and bone, stark naked, and apparently starving. The boy lunged downward and scooped up the remnant of my lunch and began to hungrily devour it. In doing so he turned his back on us and revealed a sickening sight to Goodrich and me that shocked both of us. The boy's entire rectum was hanging six to eight inches below his buttock and was bloody red. What had befallen the young man I had no way of knowing, but it seemed obvious that he would not live long without serious medical attention, which he was unlikely to receive. People moving down that sidewalk paid no attention to the youth at all. His problem was not their problem. For them life simply went on. This was one more instance of how life was in India and Pakistan. I think it was the saddest thing I can remember. French Camp had seldom seemed so far away as it did that day.

From that time on, things at Kurmitola were very routine and uneventful. During that time we even found an approximately 5-foot by 12-foot section of a cargo parachute. One of my fellow pilots, Lou Korotkin, a very promising artist, painted a picture of Snoopy from the comic strip on what we called "The Curtain," and all of our thirty-two pilots signed it. We then called in each of our three-member ground crew and had them sign it. For all the time we were in combat, it hung on a wall. Whenever important people, generals, and such came, we had them sign it. (My friend, Cecil Kramer, a recognized P-38 historian, was able to receive "The Curtain" from Vic Veroda, a great replacement pilot who brought it home. It is now displayed at all of our speeches and air show participations.)

The Curtain (Bill Behrns' collection)

We continued flying missions, but saw very little real action. The enemy was absent from the air, leaving the playing field to us to do as we wished without opposition. I can't say we weren't happy to be flying so safely, but it certainly wasn't the most interesting duty. War can be very boring at times, even for pilots.

Chapter Twenty-Seven: Early Missions in P-38H 113

On November 26, 1943, I flew 113 alongside of First Lieutenant Hampton Boggs out of Kurmitola, as we escorted a PBY on a sweep down the eastern coast of the Bay of Bengal looking for any flyers that might have been down in that area in the last few days. We were instructed, before flying any mission near coastal waters, to try to land in the bay if we knew we couldn't make it back to base since the waters were regularly patrolled by the Navy PBYs who were tasked to pick up downed pilots and any other derelict Allied personnel they might find there. Every so often, a couple of our Lightnings would escort such a mission. On this day everything was routine, and we flew our route without incident and returned to base in the late afternoon. It was usually a short mission, often in support of the Royal Air Force, but we found no one to rescue on this trip. It was 113's maiden voyage in India, and she did her job as expected.

On November 27, the Twin Dragons sent out a four-plane flight that flew into a Japanese hornet's nest, losing two pilots: Captain Armin Ortmeyer and Lieutenant Jay Harlan. Neither man was seen to fall, but both failed to return from the mission and were listed as Missing in Action.

On December 2, Lieutenant Amiel Boldman, Jr. flew along with me on an escort mission for a photo-recon F-5 (unarmed P-38 camera plane). It was rare for a "Photo Joe" to have an escort since his P-38 was faster than anything else in the sky. Without guns and ammo an F-5 weighed fully 4,000 pounds less than our H models and could easily out run us or, for that matter, anything the Japs could use against them.

Camera nose and nose art from P-38 F5 (Ken Moore photo)

Still, certain missions deep into enemy territory were deemed to be important enough to require escort. Aerial photos were of enormous importance to bombing missions that were scheduled to follow them. These pictures often contained the only hard intelligence our forces had as to the numbers and disposition of enemy units. Every effort was made to get those photos home so that the labs could develop them and get the "intel" to 10th Air Command who distributed it out to us.

Sometimes our intelligence officer, Lieutenant Morton, would show actual photos of important targets to help us orient ourselves before we attacked those sites. We usually sat close together in these meetings, already dressed for the day's action.

On December 5, 1943, ten of us escorted bombers without opposition. We were out there again escorting mediums on December 15, again without the Japs showing up. However, we did hit targets on the Rangoon-Prome rail line and also along the Irrawaddy River. These communications points were areas where much of the enemy supplies moved down the peninsula toward coastal strong points, particularly large cities like Rangoon and Mandalay. When we had "heavies" to escort, flak from the enemy was often very thick. The big B-24 Liberators had to fly "low and slow" to deliver their payloads so they were only a little better than sitting ducks once the pilot told the bombardier, "You've got the airplane." At that point, the pilot and copilot had nothing to do but sit with their arms folded across their chests or laps while the bomb man controlled the plane through his Nordern Bombsight. They flew a perfectly straight course at 150 miles per hour through the worst of the enemy fire with ten-cubic-yard patches of flying steel bursting all around, over and under them as they

Intel officer Morton gives briefing. Row 1 (right to left): Major Hampton Boggs, Lt. Arnie Thompson, Lt. Bob Hargis. Standing at center is Bill Behrns. Standing at rear is Captain Glenn. (Bill Behrns' collection)

delivered their "eggs" to target.

Up above in our P-38s, we were at least able to dodge and weave a bit to avoid black clouds of flying death. It probably did little good in all honesty, but we felt better thinking we had at least a little control of the situation. Our "big friends" had to sit there and take it, doing nothing out of necessity. I developed a strong respect for those guys who dropped down to seven thousand feet and delivered their loads in the face of such daunting resistance. In Europe, I was told, it was a whole lot worse than anything we saw from the Japs, and the casualty numbers more than bore that out. I was glad I didn't have to trade places with the bomber guys. On every mission they looked death straight in the eye and had plenty of time to study it before passing through to safety.

P-38 L (Bill Behrns' collection)

Chapter Twenty-Eight: January to February 1944

As the new year commenced, we continued flying missions out of Kurmitola. Most of these sorties were bomber-escort flights in support of B-25 medium bombers, and some others included heavy B-24s. Bomber-escort missions tended to be routine with little or no resistance from the enemy air force. On January 1st, we flew a combined escort and strafing mission that provided more interest since we got down to low levels and engaged enemy targets on the second half of the mission.

We were getting the squadron ready to move east to a base at Chittagong, but the move was postponed, and we continued with our escort missions for several more weeks. On January 20, I flew bomber escort on Captain Duke's wing. On January 23, we flew another escort mission with Captain Webb in the lead and myself flying element with Lieutenant M. P. Monrad on my wing. These missions proved to be

B-25 Mitchell Medium Bombers (Ken Moore photo)

routine flights, and all planes returned safely to base.

On February 3, things got a little rougher when I flew element wing for Lieutenant Hampton Boggs. We did both bombing and strafing that day over Okshitpin, Burma, a large city and communications hub. The Japs were moving a large group of troops and supplies through the area, and we dove down on them dropping thousand-pound bombs on the supply point. We encountered significant ground fire as we made our passes, and Lieutenant Lou Korotkin was shot down. In addition Lieutenant Burdett Goodrich was hit in an engine and flew three hundred miles home on the other Allison, becoming a member of the Lightning Christian's Club made up of those of us who owed our survival to our twin-engine fighter's ability to keep on flying after losing one mill. A fair number of us would belong to that club by the end of this deployment.

On February 9, 1944, the entire squadron traveled to Amarda Road, India, 90 miles southwest of Calcutta. There we were enrolled in a 19-day gunnery and tactics course provided by the Royal Air Force. We were provided with 16 planes in which to train once we finished ground school. Each morning we would attend classes, and when afternoon came, we flew several hours in P-38s and AT-6s.

We flew against aerial targets towed by RAF pilots. Both fighter and bomber targets were provided. While it seemed a good idea, this varied training turned out to be a little bit unnecessary since I never laid eyes on a Japanese bomber the entire time I was in Theater. Captain Luehring shot down a Betty bomber early in our Kurmitola deployment, but after that we never saw any of these highly-desirable targets. This is one reason I have always considered the record of our Twin Dragon Squadron to be so remarkable. We never once had a turkey shoot with a bunch of big, slow, defenseless bombers to shoot up at our leisure. We made our scores and our reputations on Zekes, Hamps, and Toneys, all of whom could maneuver and fight back.

School ended in satisfactory fashion, and we made ready to return to the war. Comments by RAF Wing Commander F. R. Casey DSO indicated that the Twin Dragon Fliers had absorbed the lessons of his school and predicted a bright future for the squadron. Our pilots had scored well in all exercises and had lost no flight time to maintenance problems during our nearly three weeks of training. For me, most of this had been practice of skills already learned at Muroc and Williams Field, so I experienced no difficulties. For others the instruction was necessary, and it brought our efficiency up quite a bit. Our later experiences would prove General Casey to be accurate in his assessment of our group. We were a very effective and efficient group throughout our deployment.

From here it was on to our new base at Chittagong.

Chapter Twenty-Nine: Chittagong, March 1944

March 4, 1944, marked the 459th's first mission out of our base at Chittagong. Four Lightnings, led by Captain Luehring, flew the sortie against a bridge on the Lamu River. The approach to the bridge was damaged, and the fighters destroyed five buildings. All planes returned to base.

Headquarters building and ready room at Chittagong
(Bill Behrns' collection)

March 15 found the Twin Dragons on a bombing mission during which I flew wing for flight leader Captain Webb. The Chauk Oil Fields were our target for this mission, and we carried five-hundred-pound, general-purpose bombs to drop on the target. We experienced heavy ack-ack during our runs, but the Japs scored no hits on any of our Lightnings. Since we were expecting to encounter Zeros that day, Lieutenants

Miller and Orr were assigned to fly top cover in case enemy aircraft appeared. None did, and all of us returned safely to base.

On March 16, we expected to run into aerial combat for the first time. Captains Luehring, Glen, and Webb led 14 P-38s on a sweep from Rangoon North to Prome. Our formation shot up a sawmill and several other ground targets before returning safely to base. The expected aerial resistance did not materialize.

March 19, we were back on bomber escort in support of the 490th Bomber Squadron's B-25s who were tasked to bomb the railroad and supply dumps at Wuntho. No casualties were reported to either bombers or Twin Dragon fighters.

On March 22, command of the 459th passed from Major Fouts to Captain Luehring. On that day, Captain Webb led 12 Lightnings against the Ela railroad bridge with one-thousand-pound bombs. I flew element lead in Webb's flight with Lieutenant King on my wing. The original target at Ela was obscured so we continued on to our secondary objective at Sinthe, where two other bridges were located. We dropped our bombs without visible effect to either span although the approaches to both were damaged. We flew on to the city of Chauk where we strafed targets of opportunity. There we took some ack-ack fire, but none of us were hit. All Lightnings returned safely to base.

March 25, 1944, a hastily-organized, eight-plane flight followed Lieutenant Hampton Boggs on an interception flight in the skies near Ramu. Just after 7 a.m., radar picked up an incoming bogey headed our way. This precipitated a scramble to get our Dragon flight in the air before the enemy arrived.

We all had money belts we took with us on missions since

it was not wise to leave cash around where native workers might be tempted to help themselves. Furthermore, the cash was a backup plan in case we had to parachute into the jungles where native people would likely help us get home if we could pay for that help. The Japs paid for flyers brought to them so the man with the most cash was likely to be king for the day. Once we had our belts we ran to our planes and began startup procedures. I was fourth off the ground and formed on Lieutenant Greco's wing, following Boggs and King toward the hastily-planned intercept. In the meantime, Captains Glenn and Webb formed a top cover flight over our base, flying near twenty-five thousand feet, waiting for some enemy to come into range. About 20 minutes later, Lieutenants Smith and Duke went on to join with the Boggs' flight.

The top cover flight failed to detect the approach of a Japanese twin-engine Dinah bomber that made a pass over our field dropping bombs on the runway. The bombs were small and hurt nothing, and the Dinah banked away and flew out of site beyond the nearby hills. Our high-altitude cover never saw the guy and gave no chase.

Out over Ramu, the Boggs' flight found nothing to engage and moved to nearby Dohazari, remaining there for nearly 20 minutes before being ordered to move to the chain of Central Burma Japanese Airfields on a sweep. At Shwebeo and Onbauk they once again found nothing to attack. From there the flight headed on to Japanese Headquarters at Anisakan where there were targets aplenty, both in the air, landing, and on the ground, many apparently returning from some recently-completed mission.

Lieutenant Boggs led us down to the field, sweeping across the flight line looking for targets. He was able to find several targets in a landing pattern and shot up three Hamps as they attempted to land. Boggs also got a Hamp on the ground.

Nothing presented itself as a target for me, so as Boggs pulled up from the mayhem he had caused, I followed him right straight into a flock of Zeros and Hamps. I was able to get a bead on a Hamp and poured rounds into him. The roar of machinegun fire was accented by the heavy *wump, wump, wump* of the 20 mm canon as my two-second burst went outward toward the target. I saw my tracers strike near the left wing root, but I suddenly became aware of a pair of Zekes bearing down on me from my right and slightly above. I got very busy with evasive action and shortly lost them both. Unfortunately while thus occupied I had to take my eyes off of my Hamp and did not see what finally became of him. A teammate saw me on my target and saw tracers going home, but he too became involved in survival activities and did not see a crash either. That is how you wind up with "probable"

Combat (courtesy of David Ails)

on your action report.

I pulled on up and away from my pursuers, my head on a swivel, looking everywhere at once. *Don't' forget your mirror, Bill!* Gun flashes were all over the sky, planes were pinwheeling down, and smoke was rising up from newly-made wrecks. The smell of burned cordite reached me as I sought another target, but the brief flurry of action was over for me. I looked for other planes on which to form but found no one nearby.

By this time our order was thoroughly scrambled. I had lost track of Greco some time back, and he had re-formed with Hampton Boggs. Both found themselves hotly pursued by Zeros and went into evasive maneuvers. Boggs split off to the left while Greco went right, both attempting to outrun their pursuers. Boggs managed to accomplish this feat and returned to base safely. The unfortunate Greco was never seen again.

Somewhere in the mad scramble, Lieutenant O. L. Garland shot up a Zero and was given a probable. Strangely enough, the official after-action report does not show him as being part of that mission, although it must be said that we took off in three different groups, and the original after-action report may have missed him. His victory could have been added later.

In addition, Lieutenant R. A. Hargis splashed a Hamp and Lieutenants Smith and Duke shared an Oscar between them. All in all, this was the wildest mission any of us had yet been on. It went from a scramble, to finding nothing, to being sneaked up on, to as hairy a fur ball of action as any Hollywood filmmaker could ever put on a screen. We had a total of six enemy aircraft destroyed in the air, another on the ground, and two probables. We lost two pilots, Lieutenants

Freeman and Greco. Certainly, it had been an interesting day. We were happy to go home and unwind.

The month of March concluded on a quiet note, and we moved deeper into spring before action once again demanded our attention. It has been said that war is long periods of utter boredom punctuated by brief intervals of stark terror. This is not entirely true, at least from my standpoint. I found that I had no time to be terrified while in the air. I was far too busy to contemplate my situation. Charles Lindbergh agreed with this assessment in discussing his head-on shoot down of a Sonya. "There is no fear," he said. "There is no time for it."

Under heavy stress, the soldier reverts to training, and our excellent training kept me active and intellectually uninvolved. Once again, Mr. Caradies from Hancock Aviation served as a reference, "If you have a problem don't think, react!" he said to me.

In combat you react. Thinking comes later.

Chapter Thirty: Living at Chittagong

After gunnery school, we headed to a new base about 250 miles east of Kurmitola that had recently been built. Our crewmen went back to our Kurmitola base to pack up our heavy supplies while we flew out to the new action station. It would take several days to complete the transition.

The new base we were headed toward, just outside of the city of Chittagong, was an RAF base built by U.S. Navy Sea Bees (Construction Battalion or "CB") with the intent of housing American Air Corps P-38s along with the U.S.-supplied P-47s, flown by the British. The Brit version of the big Jug did not have an automatic spark advance on the engines that British pilots were accustomed to, and on occasion, one of their pilots would try to take off before he had fully warmed his engine, (something you could do in a Hurricane or a Spitfire). He would stall out a few feet off the ground and auger into his death. The RAF did not remain with us very long, and we soon had the new digs to ourselves.

The new base at Chittagong was about a mile off the beaches of the Bay of Bengal. As a result our weather was extremely hot and humid. We spent many hours of many days hiding from the sun to get away from the one-hundred-plus-degree heat. There was no way to avoid the humidity that often matched the temperature, degree for degree. One hundred percent humidity seemed to add ten degrees to the temperature our thermometers told us we were living through, and no matter where we went the moisture came right in after us.

There was a creek that ran through camp, and some of the

guys would float around in the water on inner tubes trying to stay partially submerged and, therefore, a wee bit cooler.

The food continued to be good as our resident butcher soon cultivated the local farmers and fishermen, and we continued to eat very well with plenty of fresh meat and vegetables.

We added to the table fare by hunting in the nearby grasslands where we could bag creatures we called "barking deer," so named because of the "oof, oof, oof" sound they made when startled. These animals were smaller than our American species, 40 pounds being pretty big, but the hindquarters were meaty and very delicious. Large areas of the valley floor were covered with tall, dense "elephant grass" which was traversed by numerous animal trails, and it was there we went to find prey for our table. We hunted the deer at night by the light of jeep headlights, aided by a moveable spotlight we mounted atop the vehicle. One of us would shoot at the eyes that glowed back at us from the grass while the other kept the lights on the target. We could usually bag two or three deer in an evening without straying too far from camp, so some of us went out quite often.

On one such evening safari, I was paired with Arnold Thompson from New Jersey. We did a lot of things together while in India, and I doubt I had a better friend in the squadron than Arnie. We were driving slowly through elephant grass along an animal trail when I spotted an eye, just one, staring out at us. I jammed on the brakes, stopped the jeep and pointed out the objective to Arnie, who dismounted the vehicle and moved around to the front where he could shoot while I directed the overhead spotlight. Arnie raised the light .25 caliber carbine he carried to his shoulder and squeezed the trigger for a shot. There followed a loud click as the hammer fell on an empty chamber. Arnie mouthed a smelly, four-letter expletive and worked the action for a fresh round, hoping the target would not move away due to all the clanking of machinery. As he raised the rifle again the target eye moved slightly to our right and another spot lit up about ten inches to the left. The eyes burned at us like small fires. "Uh oh!" Arnie said as he scrambled back into the jeep. "Get us out of here, Bill. NOW!"

I backed the jeep up slowly trying not to upset the tiger that was staring at us. We managed a few yards before a quick bootlegger turn got us out of the area. Facing a Bengal tiger with a popgun was not our idea of a fun evening. I have often wondered what would have happened if Arnie had properly loaded his gun in the first place. Perish the thought! Thank God for a miss-fire.

Tiger from painting by Tina Moore

Chapter Thirty-One: Showers, Latrines, & Other Mundane Things

Keeping ourselves clean and healthy was a matter of constant concern among the pilots of the 459th Fighter Squadron. We were living in hot, humid conditions that demanded a daily shower at minimum and a great deal of attention to the maintenance of our hands, feet, and particularly our teeth. We constructed shower facilities by using 55-gallon fuel drums, fortunately available in large numbers. We removed the top of a steel drum and welded a spigot, which could be turned on and off on the bottom, near the center, where we wanted the water. Workers added water from above by the bucketful, which they carried up a ladder. We had a warm, if not hot shower whenever we wanted one. A cold shower was not possible in the tropical region, but no one ever complained about that.

We got water from a clear running stream that passed through the camp a few yards away from the shower stands. This water was relatively clean for being from a natural source in a third-world country. Our squadron history talked about using polluted water from ponds for this purpose, but I felt we did pretty well given what we had available. Nothing here was truly clean unless boiled or otherwise artificially sterilized, so we used the best source we could since purification was a major task. None of us came down with anything ugly because of shower water.

There was little privacy for the bather, but we really didn't care about it. Modesty was a wonderful thing when conditions allowed for it, but with a front-line unit like the

459th FS, there was no time for it. You disrobed and washed yourself while those who wished to watched. Most of us didn't bother. Some showers actually had tarps wrapped around them. Some did not.

Military units in the field have done this kind of thing in every war within national memory as long as the troops were in one place long enough to consider it a base. It was a Ma and Pa Kettle solution to our problem, but it worked well enough to keep us clean and healthy. Marjorie Maine would have been proud of us.

Running water was an ultimate luxury in that part of the world, generally available only in the really major cities like Rangoon or Calcutta. The only base I occupied in India or Burma that had a full water system was Kurmitola, which was very close to the major city of Dacca. There we had running water, which was a major luxury for us. In other places, water had to be carried before it could be used. Hot water was heated over wood fires and then carried to cast iron tubs for baths if you were lucky enough to be in a place that had such things. Out in the sticks, we never encountered this level of hygiene. We made do with creek and pond water and 55-gallon drums.

Defecation problems were handled in traditional infantry style, using a long, open slit trench with no privacy at all. We simply mooned the world, and let it fly. Every so often our workers would fill in the trench and dig a new one, and the process would begin again. George Washington would have been comfortable here. It was just like home in Valley Forge, only 90 degrees hotter.

We paid great attention to our feet, particularly the areas between our toes. There were various forms of fungus and several nasty parasites that caused people problems unlikely to be encountered stateside. We also brushed our teeth vigorously and often for the same reasons. Gum disease was rampant in the native population, and we wanted no part of what we saw in some of our on-base workers.

In general, the Twin Dragons stayed healthy, losing very little time to hospitalization due to things other than wounds suffered in combat. Once again our excellent training came through for us. We were taught what to do and drilled until behavior became habit. Some things "military" work pretty well and our regimen of cleanliness was one of them.

There was one thing that did cause us a lot of trouble, and that was malaria. Malaria is carried by female mosquitos, which thrive in areas with large amounts of standing, rather than running, water. In India and Pakistan, standing water is almost everywhere. It is difficult to protect yourself against these flying insects regardless of the many precautions you may take to do so. One or more of the pesky biters will somehow get through. Many of our pilots came down with this debilitating disease and lost airtime because of it. The stuff was rampant at Chittagong, and the 459th was once again at half-strength, this time because of flying insects rather than lack of flyable P-38s.

Somehow I managed to escape the ravages of tropical disease. Perhaps the reason was the same one that helped me to avoid the usual childhood diseases suffered by children at home other than me. Goat's milk rules! What else could it have been?

Keeping cool was another problem on one-hundred-degree-plus days laced with extreme humidity. We often spent time floating in the creek or nearby pond supported by float bags just so we could be submerged in water and maybe ten degrees cooler. The creek was preferred because it was nearer, and running water was cleaner. We came to appreciate the habits of water buffalos that must submerge themselves in cool water four hours or more a day if they are to survive the constant heat. While we were not that vulnerable, we definitely understood the idea and tried to copy it to some extent. Pilots as mermaids. Who would have guessed?

Mermaids (Bill Behrns' collection)

Chapter Thirty-Two: April 1944

On April 18, we escorted B-24s to bomb oil installations at Yenanyaung. It was my birthday, so I remember the day better than most. The mission was uneventful except for one Hamp who seemed to want to play, doing aerobatics in what was probably an attempt to lure our Lightnings into a trap. We ignored the Nip, as Major Webb ordered, and went on to our target where the "heavies" delivered their ordinance,low and slow like usual. We then turned back the way we had come to return to base.

There was a solid cloud cover at about ten thousand feet, which made observation difficult, and this shortly proved to be a problem. As I was swivel-heading about seeking Japs I glanced in my rear view mirror, and suddenly, from out of that cloud cover, there he was right behind me. The Jap's engine cowl completely filled my mirror. He was very, very close, and there were tracers spouting from the plane and passing on both sides of me. I immediately dove down and left as sharply as I could and firewalled the engines. My insides were totally in an uproar as I felt multiple bullet impacts on my plane. My evasive move got me clear somehow, and I was able to flatten out into normal flight before I took stock of my situation by visually inspecting my Lightning. To my left, an oil slick was forming on the engine cowl indicating I had taken a hit to an oil line or cooler, so I immediately shut down my left engine and feathered the prop. Still flying, still unhurt, I felt I could make it home.

In the meantime the gloves were off for the rest of the squadron, who immediately engaged the enemy fighter. Our pilots, eight of them, made efforts to catch this guy, but we were never able to hook onto him. No other Japs appeared, and we all returned to base. I trailed a thin wisp of smoke for the whole two hundred miles, but other than that, the trip was routine. Lightnings flew very well on one engine. I cruised home at 250 miles per hour doing S-turns to stay with our bombers. It was a 30-minute flight with my right-hand Allison happily singing its power song as if nothing unusual was happening.

When I got back on the ground, Al Kocher and Wayne Sneddon examined my plane and found over a hundred various battle scars on her, including several bullet holes and one severed oil line that fed the left-hand Allison. My quick shutdown had saved the motor, and Al had the plane ready for the next mission.

On this day, we began receiving 12 new P-38Js, ferried up to us from Dum Dum Field in Calcutta, bringing our squadron back up to full strength. We had been whittled down to 13 available Lightnings. Our squadron had been down to half strength and operating at full blast. A Unit Citation was issued a few months later describing this situation and commending the 459th for maintaining full military operations with less than full equipment.

I was one of the lucky pilots who received a P-38J from this shipment. I was happy to have a newer model fighter since the J's were both more powerful and easier to fly due to improvements made by Lockheed. It was also a fresh horse, having never before been assigned a permanent pilot. The occasion caused me to initiate a conversation with my crew chief, Al Kocher, and we came up with a name and developed a design for nose art on our new Lightning.

I told Al to start with the idea of a Lightning Bolt suggested by the popular name of the P-38. Astride the yellow bolt would be a mostly-naked young lass wearing shorts and black boots and holding a pair of reins in black-gloved hands with which she could control her mount. Her nakedness from the waist up was neatly concealed by the position of her arms as she reached out to hold the reins, leaving the more intimate parts of her anatomy to the imagination of the viewer. Trailing behind her head was a wave of long black hair flying in the motion-generated wind.

Since I hailed from San Joaquin County, I decided to name her the *San Joaquin Siren*. The name had a good sound to it and was easy to remember. A tech sergeant, who was an artist, painted the character on the nose. He then added my name as pilot. Other than that, the only noteworthy marking was the big white number 8 on the outside surface of each vertical stabilizer.

Other pilots chose plane names for a variety of reasons including girlfriends' or wives' names, cartoon characters, movie heroes, and on ad infinitum. Others chose as I did and developed names based on geographic references, usually in their home localities.

Nose art on the San Joaquin Siren (courtesy of David Ails)

One such example was from Lieutenant Harry H. Sealy from Hawaii, who named his P-38 Haleakala, after the world's most famous and most active volcano located just a few miles from his home. The name seemed appropriate since both the volcano and the Lightning spit fire on numerous occasions.

Ten days later, on April 28, I flew my first mission in the

Siren. Along with three others I was on Red Alert. We would be sent into the air to protect our base should the need arise. At 11:30 a.m., newly promoted Captain Walter Duke took a flight of four up looking for incoming fighters. I was on Goodrich's wing in the Charlie spot while Lieutenant William Baumeister flew wing for Duke. We found nothing to engage and returned to base. Later in the afternoon Captain Duke and Lieutenant Goodrich made another sortie but came up empty again.

The next day, April 29, at 1535 hours, Captain Max Glenn led a 21-plane sortie bound for Augbong where no enemy planes were found. Focus of the mission turned to the base at Heho. Four of our Lightnings developed engine trouble, and Captain Glenn, being one of them, led that flight home. Captains Broadfoot and Duke took over command of the flight, and we continued onward.

Lt. Bill Behrns seated in brand new San Joaquin Siren
(Bill Behrns' collection)

Heho failed to produce so we continued on to Meiktila where we found everything airborne. There were 20 or so enemy planes in the air over that base, and Captain Duke led us straight through the horde of enemy fighters in front of us.

We found targets in all directions and began to spread out. A flight of four aircraft in that situation tends to move apart from each other to provide maneuvering room and clear fields of fire. As we began to loosen up our four-pack, targets began to present themselves. I found a target about half-way through, coming up on an Oscar from behind. I hammered him hard as my gunsight came to bear. The concentrated pattern of P-38 bullets tore the target in pieces. The Oscar exploded into a huge fireball, which I flew straight through, hoping the remnants of enemy fighter would be somewhere beneath me. Fire tended to rise while steel would normally fall unless propelled by the blast. I felt no impacts passing through, and gun camera photos confirmed the kill for me on return to base. The *San Joaquin Siren* had scored her first victory.

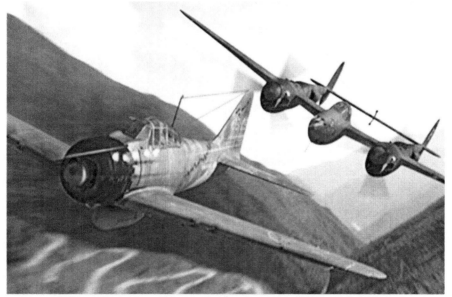

The Siren on his tail (courtesy of David Ails)

Captain Duke also got an Oscar, and Lieutenant Goodrich chopped up another Oscar that was smoking on the way down. While no one saw it hit the ground, Goodrich was later credited with a kill on that plane. Lieutenant Bearden also collected an Oscar for his score sheet. Once again a minute or two had provided all of the action. Two of our Lightnings suffered bullet holes, but everyone returned to base in good order.

Later that evening, Tokyo Rose came on the radio and talked directly to our unit and Wally Duke in particular. "You did well today, Captain Duke," she said, "but we are coming, and we will get you tomorrow."

It was only five hours after we had returned from our mission, and the enemy capital already knew. April passed into history, and we moved on into May.

THE UNITED STATES OF AMERICA

TO ALL WHO SHALL SEE THESE PRESENTS, GREETING.

THIS IS TO CERTIFY THAT
THE PRESIDENT OF THE UNITED STATES OF AMERICA
AUTHORIZED BY ACT OF CONGRESS, JULY 2, 1926,
HAS AWARDED

THE DISTINGUISHED FLYING CROSS

TO
FIRST LIEUTENANT WILLIAM M. BEHRNS
ARMY OF THE UNITED STATES
FOR HEROISM
WHILE PARTICIPATING IN AERIAL FLIGHT

ON 29 APRIL 1944 IN BURMA

GIVEN UNDER MY HAND IN THE CITY OF WASHINGTON
THIS 20TH DAY OF JANUARY 2010

The Distinguished Flying Cross awarded to Bill Behrns on April 29, 1944

Chapter Thirty-Three: May 1944

May 5, 1944, I was involved in two separate missions, a bomber escort and a fighter sweep. We took off under the lead of Captain Webb to rendezvous with British Wellingtons for a bombing mission at Tiddim, Burma. This turned out to be a bust as we circled the contact area for 20 minutes and saw no planes to escort. We returned to base, empty-handed and more than a little disappointed. It was not unusual to miss connections with bomber formations. In Europe, it happened often due to weather in which bombers decided at the last minute not to fly. In those situations the fighter escorts were already in route and could not be contacted. Oftentimes, these snafus led to impromptu search-and-destroy missions that could be very productive. At other times, like this one, we escorts returned to base empty handed and waited for the next assignment.

In the afternoon, 1600 hours, Captain Glenn took a ten-plane group on a sweep of Anisakan. We climbed to twenty-five thousand feet and headed for the now well-known target area. As we approached our target, we dropped down to fifteen thousand feet and dropped our external tanks preparatory to action. Unfortunately, there was no one to attack at that site, so we continued on with the goal of returning to base.

On the way home, Captain Duke went looking for targets of opportunity, and I was included in his flight. We dove on a building complex near Monywa and started several fires, one in a particularly large building. As we passed over the target, I felt an impact on the right side of the *Siren* and looked over to see my right engine smoking copiously from what

An outdoor briefing by Lt. Burdette Goodrich. Bill is kneeling near the map (Bill Behrns' collection)

later turned out to be oil line damage. I feathered the Allison quickly and continued on with my one remaining engine running strong and smooth.

A P-38 is quite flyable on only one of her two Allison engines. The plane is capable of four hundred miles per hour on a single mill and can cruise above twenty-five thousand feet in that condition. We seldom worried about single-engine flight unless the remaining engine also showed problems. Many of us made our way home after losing an engine to the enemy or to other causes. Engine problems were more common in P-38s than they were in P-47s or P-51s, probably because there was twice the opportunity in Lightnings. Still, it should be noted that pilots seldom complained about engine trouble in Mustangs or Jugs, probably because such pilots seldom made it back to base.

A story about this situation comes to us from the 475th FS, an all P-38 group, where a pilot remembered receiving a radio call while returning from a mission to Rabaul. "I'm losing coolant, and my temperature is going up. What do I do?" the call said.

"Hell," the Lightning driver replied, "feather it and fly home."

"Feather it, hell," the reply came back, "I'm flying a P-51."

Point made. Twenty-nine times during our deployment with the 459th, pilots flew home safely on one engine, saving both airplane and pilot to fight another day. I managed this feat six different times myself. The Lightning Christian's Club was alive and well in Burma.

I got back to base without incident and turned the *Siren* over to my crew chief, Al Kocher, to see if he could get her ready for the next assignment. One of the secrets of any fighter pilot's success be he hot, cold, or just lucky to be alive, is the efficiency of his ground crew and the crew chief in particular. A first-rate crew chief was the man who kept his plane flying and kept his pilot in the air. (Make no mistake about it: both pilot and plane belonged to the crew chief.) In my case, my man, Al Kocher, was the best of the best. I never had a single incidence of airplane trouble in one hundred missions and other types of more casual flying. My Lightnings ran sweet and strong under the competent care of this tough sergeant from Texas. Long after the war, Al would remember being proud of seeing his P-38 come in with an engine shot out and having her ready to fly on the very next mission. Al had to accomplish this Herculean task a half dozen times, and he never failed to have my *Siren* ready for me when my turn came to fly. We suffered no downtime during my entire deployment. Also deserving thanks for this considerable achievement was our Lockheed Technical Representative, Wayne Sneddon, who found necessary parts and incorporated updates as they became available. The *San Joaquin Siren* was always on the cutting edge. Everything was right. The rest was up to me.

On May 7, 1944, we made a fighter sweep with Captain Duke leading our flight and Captain Glenn in overall command. Lieutenant Broadfoot could not get off the ground and stayed put. Several planes returned home with engine problems, and one plane got lost in the shuffle and came home to regroup. Our flight under Captain Duke continued on to target where he caught the Japanese in a landing pattern. Duke scored an Oscar in the process. Lieutenants Bearden and Hargis scored an Oscar apiece. This brought the Twin Dragon Score up to ninety-six aircraft destroyed including both air and ground kills.

On May 8, I took the *Siren* in Captain Duke's flight with Burdett Goodrich on my wing. The group shot up two Oscars, but both escaped, smoking but flying. No good scores for us that day.

May 10, Captain Duke took eight Lightnings out to Imphal, where reports had forty enemy planes operating. This was a promising bag of Nips, and if we could get the jump on them we might well bring down several. Duke decided to try a little slight of hand on the Japs and flew directly over Shwebo where our formation was sure to be seen and reported. He led us on for nearly a hundred miles or about fifteen minutes flying time and then turned abruptly south and came at the enemy from there. We caught the Japs on the ground as we had hoped we would, and we streaked across the field wide open with little opposition ahead of us. Our battle line shot up three planes on the ground and also tore apart several small hangers where additional planes were probably parked. The Duke flight boosted our total to ninety-eight destroyed with four more probables in burning hangers. On this run, Captain Duke scored another Oscar and shared another with Lieutenant Burger, who also got an Oscar of his own. All of us returned safely to base. May was fast becoming a productive month.

Miss V, piloted by Captain Walter Duke. Duke was CBI's only American double ace (courtesy 459th Fighter Squadron)

Things calmed down a bit for next few days, and it would be May 17 before the Twin Dragons again appeared in the air. Major Luehring took out 20 planes toward Rangoon for the Hmawbi base and on to Kanguang. There was little success to report, one Oscar damaged on the ground. The guys were disappointed, but we made ready to go out again two days later.

On May 19, I rode the *Siren* out with Major Luehring on a sixteen-plane sweep toward Shwebo, two hundred fifty miles from Chittagong, where a large airfield was located. We visited that site quite often looking for targets of opportunity.

I was paired with Captain Glenn and followed him as he engaged an Oscar and shot that plane up badly. I found an Oscar quite close by and went after him, scoring several hits and causing that plane to nose over and fall straight down into the jungle below.

On returning to base, I found that Goodrich had been credited with an Oscar and Duke had also collected an Oscar. I called on Major Luehring and told him about my Oscar, but I was unable to convince him that I had shot down that plane. "Did anyone else see it go in?" he asked me.

"Some of the guys saw me hit him, but none of them saw the crash," I replied.

"Well, did it burn on impact?" Luehring asked.

"Not that I saw," I answered. "It went nose down into the bush, and that was it."

The commandant looked off into space for a moment and then said, "If you can fly me out there and show me the wreck it's your kill. Otherwise, it's got to be a probable." That ended our conversation on the subject. Since there were no noticeable landmarks, and the plane apparently didn't burn, I doubted I could find that place in that thick jungle if I had a week to do it. Captain Glenn also was given a probable for the same reasons.

While I'm not sure the decision was entirely fair, there was no doubt that it was even-handed. Major Luehring was very much a 'letter of the law' man when it came to the rules of confirmation. If wing cameras (not very effective, especially on deflection shots) or no other pilot reported seeing it crash, you did not get a victory. He was even hard on himself that way, giving himself only three air-to-air wins. I would think about this situation often in the coming months and eventually came to some conclusions I will discuss at length later on.

On May 23, we were in action again, launching two separate sorties from our base. I flew with Captain Glenn on the 16-plane afternoon flight to Meiktila for targets of opportunity. I was flying wing for Lieutenant Burdett Goodrich as the second element in Captain Duke's flight. We employed our special Twin Dragon attack by diving full out on the field from altitude, passing over the target at four hundred miles per hour in a long line of battle. It was necessary to make our passes in single file to avoid collisions and to minimize the chance of shooting down a friendly. This gave the enemy ground soldiers a good opportunity to fire on us and, on occasion, some of us took hits. I escaped that problem this time, but Lieutenant Garland returned to base on one engine with several bullet holes in his ship.

I was again paired with Captain Walt Duke as we ran the gauntlet of enemy fire and pulled up looking for targets in the air. I found an Oscar directly in front of me just as Captain Duke was lining up on one to our right. I was unaware of Duke's action as I was riveted on my own target. My gunsight came to bear, and I poured a heavy, two-second burst into the Oscar in front of me and saw Holy Hell envelop that airplane. From the rear, our 20-millimeter canon shells could pass completely through a flying target assuming they did not explode inside the plane, which they often did. The pilot was likely dead before fire broke out all over the Oscar, which nosed over and plunged downward crashing heavily to earth beneath a canopy of tall trees. I did not see the impact myself, but a squadron mate verified the crash later on. At any rate, I had rare gun camera confirmation, so no one contested this one. In the meantime, Captain Duke had destroyed his Oscar, and we both returned to base happy with our efforts.

On May 25, the Squadron mourned the loss of Second Lieutenant W. R. Lyon to an accident of undetermined cause. Lyon was flying out to begin a mission under direction of Captain Luehring when his plane slowed and then dove into the ground from ten thousand feet. Several radio calls failed to get a response, and no one was ever able to explain what happened. We lost a good man and a good friend to no good reason. Such is war. Soldier on.

May 30, 1944, two sorties were flown. At 10:20 in the morning, Captain Glenn took six planes on a sweep including me in my *Siren*. We encountered nothing of interest and returned safely to base. Major Luehring took eight planes out in the afternoon and also returned without incident.

May 31 saw the Twin Dragons escorting bombers on a routine mission. I flew with Captain Broadfoot and returned to base unharmed, as we encountered no significant opposition. The merry Month of May was behind us, and the monsoon season lurked directly ahead.

Chapter Thirty-Four: June 6, 1944

On June 6, our Twin Dragons began a 20-plane fighter sweep aimed at Meiktila airfield, 278 miles from Chittagong. The pilots were excited about the mission since there was a very good possibility that we would encounter enemy fighters and get the chance for some more victories. Little did we know what kind of day this would turn out to be.

We jumped off at 0630 hours and headed off in groups of four. Two planes turned back quite early due to engine trouble, and the remaining 18 moved on toward the target. The lead flight was composed of Major Luehring with Lieutenant Robert Hargis on his wing and Lieutenant Burdett Goodrich with me as his wingman. Farther back was a flight composed of Captain Walter Duke with Lieutenant William Baumeister as his wingman. Element lead in the Duke group fell to Lieutenant Oscar Garland with Lieutenant William Orr riding shotgun for him in the Charlie spot. The order of battle would become important later in the day.

We arrived over the target area in good order and shook ourselves out into a line to make our passes. Major Luehring went first, diving down, Dragon Style, firing as he went. Hargis came through next, about half a mile back of the major. As he dropped down into the fight, Goodrich and I lined ourselves up and got some space between us for our four-hundred-mile-per-hour, low-level pass across the field.

There wasn't a whole lot to shoot at on the ground this day as the Nips apparently had prior knowledge of our approach and had nearly everything flyable in the air by the time we arrived. As it turned out there was at least one Zeke still on the ground, although no one reported seeing it or shooting at it on the first pass.

We soon found out where those absent planes were as Luehring and Hargis flew up into a swarm of Oscars and Zeros as they climbed out from their gun runs. Goodrich and I spotted this crowd of hostiles trying to get lined up on the squadron leaders, so rather than attempt to fly directly through what appeared to be a very lively hornet's nest, we stayed low and powered our way past the threat, very near to the ground. We literally buzzed our way to safety.

Having escaped ground fire unscathed and outrun the Japanese top cover, Goodrich and I swung wide around to the left, lining up for another pass at the target. Goodrich was a ways in front of me and began his turn first. Seeing what he was up to, I also turned left and, due to our respective positions, I was able to turn inside of him and bring the *Siren* toward the enemy more quickly. I found myself now in the lead position with Goodrich behind me, exactly the reverse of the way we were when we first went through.

As I passed by the airfield, heading toward the menacing cloud of Nip fighters, I noticed an Oscar a short distance in front of me, coming up off the field on takeoff. The pilot was apparently looking at something other than me, as he did not react to the presence of my *Siren* lurking behind and to his left. He was climbing and had his wings turned, banking just slightly above and ahead of me, looking for a P-38 that his radio had just said was close by. He apparently was looking straight ahead as the *Siren* moved up on his left and slightly behind him. As I approached the Oscar, I was directly in line with the crown of his canopy, right above his head in a definite blind spot.

Since I was still at speed I had to turn hard right to get a

Behrns-Sumino combat, June 6, 1944 (courtesy of David Ails)

line on this bogey before flying right past him, which would have put me in a very vulnerable position. The best I could get was a thirty-degree deflection shot for about two seconds. Even then I could not shoot directly at the Oscar, so I treated him like a fast-flying mallard from the San Joaquin Valley. I shot in front of him, hanging a lead fence directly in his path. I stayed on the trigger until I saw his engine and canopy in my sight.

As the sight came to bear, I saw the Oscar's canopy fly off the plane as my tracers hit home from the propeller back to the pilot. The fighter caught fire and angled down toward the ground streaming flames. I flew behind and over my fifth kill and kept going. There were many more Zeros and Oscars around, and I did not need to miss seeing one like number five had missed me.

At that moment I heard a radio call from Goodrich saying just two words. "I'll verify," he said from somewhere behind me. I did not answer but straightened out and made for open skies. It was time to head home, as the rest of the squadron seemed to be doing.

When I landed at Chittagong nearly an hour later, I told my crew chief, Al Kocher, to paint another rising sun flag on the *Siren* because I had downed another Jap, and Lieutenant Goodrich would be along any minute to verify it. Al got

Burma Road Victory (courtesy of David Ails)

right to it and soon had the flag in place. Unfortunately my friend Burdette Goodrich did not return to base, having been shot down just after his radio call to me. I did not get my confirmation that day. I remember mentioning my shoot down to Hampton Boggs shortly after landing, so I know someone in the inner circle knew of my claim. Later I approached Captain Luehring with that information but was never credited with so much as a probable. After that, Goodrich would be credited with shooting down "a fighter," although he never claimed one, and I never heard of anyone verifying a claim. How this came about will be discussed in the following chapter.

It was quite a while before we found out what had befallen Lieutenant Goodrich. Lieutenant Baumeister was reported to have seen him go down, although I fail to see how that might have happened given the order of battle that day. Baumeister had been part of the Duke flight and would have cleared the area before Goodrich and I came through a second time. Nonetheless, that is how the record reads. The report containing this information came from a source on the ground back in Chittagong, and I was never able to verify its accuracy.

Someone, most likely Lieutenant William Baumeister, who reported seeing Goodrich go down, said he got out of his crashed plane okay, which later proved to be true. He no sooner did that than a native partisan shot him through the left side of his neck, just missing a kill shot. It is not known if Goodrich was resisting or simply standing alone when the rice farmer shot him. It is known that the farmer was paid by the Japanese for turning over an American flyer to them as a prisoner. Goodrich was taken to a nearby POW camp where he was treated for his wound. He died a short time later.

As a result of radio calls from Baumeister, Captain Walter Duke returned to the area in search of Goodrich or perhaps Baumeister, his now-absent wingman. Duke never returned from that sortie, and what became of him was never conclusively determined.

After the war Major Boggs did research involving "Japanese Intelligence sources." His subsequent report said that the Japanese had waited until the Americans had left the area and apparently only Captain Duke was left. They had then engaged him and shot him down. In the process these sources indicated that Duke had shot down three Japanese before they destroyed him. These "victories" were submitted as a claim for Duke based on Japanese reports. The Pentagon never accepted them. No such Japanese Intelligence report exists in the Tokyo Archives of the Japanese Army Air Force, as research done on my behalf many years later has conclusively proven. Those same archives confirm the time, place, and circumstance of my victory, as a letter from a Japanese researcher proves with no room for doubt. It took me sixty-six years to get credit for what I did that day, and without the help of several important people both here and in Japan, I would still be waiting.

As I later found out, the man I shot down over Meiktila was Captain Goichi Sumino, the leading Japanese ace in CBI. He was credited with twenty-seven victories (some shared), and was the last Great Ace of Japan in our area of war. He was apparently playing "GO" with the base commander when our P-38s appeared over the field and, though wounded in his left arm at the time, he left his game and climbed into his commander's Oscar and went up in defense of his base, flying right into the guns of the *San Joaquin Siren* as he did so. As is common in such aerial combats, the entire episode was over in seconds. Captain Sumino never had a chance to engage with the enemy (me) before it was over for him. I was well inside 150 yards when our paths crossed, and my lead fence was too tall for him to jump. Research into past aerial wars from WWI onward shows this pattern to be the dominant feature of air-to-air combat. Most often the pilot does not see the man who kills him. It just happens, and the rest is history.

Thinking back on it after so many years, it occurs to me that Captain Sumino was very likely the pilot who avoided eight P-38s a few months before on December 12th, 1943.

We first observed him flying off to the side of our path doing circles, loops, and rolls, trying to attract our attention. Captain Sealy ordered us not to engage that plane, as it was likely a decoy to lure us away from the bombers. Later on, that same plane dropped out of the high overcast and came in on me from above, shooting out my right engine before I could get away from him. The entire squadron then went after him, but no one was able to get a good shot at him. That pilot was a master of aerobatics and flew through the group as if it was no problem to avoid seasoned combat pilots in very capable aircrafts. We didn't get him that day, but pilots can only go out so often before fate and Lightnings catch up with them.

Captain Sumino may very well have claimed me as one of his shoot-downs since I left the area trailing smoke from a shot-up oil line, but I made it home okay. In the end, it was I who shot him down. Such are the fortunes of war.

Most of the Japanese Great Aces did not survive the war. The Japs did not have sufficient numbers available to replace their best people at the end of one or two tours of duty. Those pilots started flying combat in 1936 and stayed until they either died or the war ended. Most did not last until the end.

As an after-action gesture, I packed Burdette Goodrich's gear in his footlocker and prepared it for delivery to the States. Good friends took care of such things.

Many years later, Burdette's younger brother, also a pilot, put together an expedition of sorts to discover what had happened to his brother and others who were in that prison camp. The expedition was lengthy and exhaustive as the searchers tracked the final disposition of the 57 bodies recovered in late 1945 by the U.S. military from the cemetery associated with this detention facility. Some were American and many others were British. The remains were loaded aboard a C-47 and flown out with the intention of landing in Calcutta. Along the way, the flight encountered inclement weather and subsequently disappeared with all hands and cargo.

We never found out where the plane went down. Resulting searches produced no traces of wreckage associated with that flight. A treasure trove of forensic evidence was now lost to us. If the plane crashed in the jungle perhaps it will be discovered someday and a multitude of family questions in many parts of our world could be answered. It is more likely, however, that the plane went down in the Bay of Bengal and is lost to us forever. It was a noble effort that came to an unfortunate end.

The effect of the June 6 action on our squadron was profound. We had lost two aces in one day and had only one lone shoot down to show for the sacrifice. It was difficult to imagine the loss of both Duke and Goodrich on the same mission. The confusion that followed is, perhaps, understandable as the Twin Dragons struggled to adjust and cover our losses. Still, a proper investigation would have uncovered much necessary information, but no such effort was ever undertaken to my knowledge. June 6, 1944, was our worst day in World War Two.

[ ] (   )
Office of the Operations Officer
APO # 433

6 June 1944

OPERATIONS ORDER)

NUMBER   118)

1. The following combat missions will be conducted this date:

MISSION NO.	T.O.	TYPE	A/C NO.	PILOT	MISSION BASIC	LOCAL
147	0510	P-38J	42-67288	1st Lt W C Orr	C	Weather Recon.
148	0615	P-38J	42-67627	Major V D Luehring	C	Fighter Sweep
148	0615	P-38J	42-67286	1st Lt R A Hargis	C	Fighter Sweep
148	0615	P-38H	42-67001	1st Lt B C Goodrich	C	Fighter Sweep
148	0615	P-38J	42-67293	1st Lt W M Behrns	C	Fighter Sweep
148	0615	P-38J	42-104154	Capt H E Boggs	C	Fighter Sweep
148	0615	P-38H	42-66982	2nd Lt J L Huesmann	C	Fighter Sweep
148	0615	P-38J	42-67292	1st Lt J C Harris	C	Fighter Sweep
148	0615	P-38H	42-67004	2nd Lt R E Fertig	C	Fighter Sweep
148	0615	P-38J	42-67632	Major M H Glenn	C	Fighter Sweep
148	0615	P-38J	42-67291	1st Lt E L Barnes	C	Fighter Sweep
148	0615	P-38J	42-67834	1st Lt H R Mahler	C	Fighter Sweep
148	0615	P-38J	42-67842	Capt W C Broadfoot	C	Fighter Sweep
148	0615	P-38H	42-67009	2nd Lt P A Jarvis	C	Fighter Sweep
148	0615	P-38J	42-66979	1st Lt I F Klumb	C	Fighter Sweep
148	0615	P-38J	42-67626	Capt W F Duke	C	Fighter Sweep
148	0615	P-38H	42-67008	2nd Lt W C Baumeister Jr	C	Fighter Sweep
148	0615	P-38H	42-66980	1st Lt O L Garland	C	Fighter Sweep
148	0615	P-38J	42-67288	1st Lt W C Orr	C	Fighter Sweep
149	1355	P-38J	42-67627	Capt W C Broadfoot	C	Search Mission
149	1355	P-38H	42-67009	2nd Lt P A Jarvis	C	Search Mission
149	1355	P-38J	42-104154	Capt R A Campbell	C	Search Mission
149	1355	P-38H	42-66979	1st Lt H R Mahler	C	Search Mission
149	1355	P-38J	42-67293	2nd Lt W C Baumeister Jr	C	Search Mission
149	1355	P-38H	42-66989	F/O D E Sowder	C	Search Mission
149	1355	P-38J	42-67291	1st Lt E L Barnes	C	Search Mission
149	1355	P-38J	42-67286	2nd Lt J L King	C	Search Mission

By order of MAJOR LUEHRING:

Harry H. Sealy

HARRY H. SEALY,
1st Lt., Air Corps,
Asst Operations Officer.

Operations order June 6, 1944. This was the order of battle as we began our June 6 mission.

Chapter Thirty-Five: R and R in Srinagar

Shortly after our June 6 mission, I flew the *Siren* down to Srinagar in Kashmir. Three of us made a mini-formation on the way down: Lieutenant Robert Brown, Lieutenant Arnold Thompson, and me. We found the airport on the edge of the city and shook ourselves into a line for landing, parking our Lightnings as directed. We then headed into town.

This large city is one of the oldest and most spectacular locations in the world. It was a favorite spot for American pilots when we took our Rest and Relaxation (R and R) leave, which came up for us during the monsoon season when little consequential flying could be done. Our side went inactive and so did the enemy during this season of constant downpours, so it was a good time to head north and west to Kashmir.

Srinagar is a combination of two Sanskrit words that together mean "wealthy city." The metropolis lives up to its name featuring an unusual blend of cultural influences not found in other major Indian (now Kashmir) cities. The original settlement may have been founded by King Ashoka or perhaps by Emperor Ashoka (different people, different tribes) or by a later ruler who may have been Pushtin. There is some confusion involved in determining the origin of this city, but no one argues its beauty, diversity, and unique industries. Emperor Ashoka introduced Buddhism into the valley. The Huns arrived in the 6th century A.D., and not long after that, Islam began to flourish here also. Around 1814, Raja Rasnit Singh brought the Sikh religion to Srinagar, and devotees of that belief set themselves up as a buffer between

Buddhists and Muslims and the now-common Christians in the area. Add Hindus to the mix and you begin to see all sorts of chances for abject chaos. Such is not the case in the "wealthy city." Srinagar is peaceful, happy, and very wealthy. The culture there is hundreds, if not thousands of years old, and everyone gets along and respects the beliefs of others including the tourists. WWII raged nearly everywhere in the CBI except here.

The airport at Srinagar lies right on the edge of town, and once the three of us had deplaned, we headed straight into the city to make our contacts for the next leg of our journey out to Dal Lake. We had booked a stay on one of the lake's many famous houseboats and were looking forward to an enjoyable time away from the stresses of war.

For that area of the world, the Dal Lake houseboats were close to the ultimate luxury. The boats were 60 feet long and 30 feet wide with double decks, 3 bedrooms, excellent dining rooms and bath areas, and features and fixtures that were the stuff of dreams. Tables and chairs were hand carved out of pure, solid black walnut. Ornate hand carved figures and patterns covered many of the surfaces and all of the supporting legs. The furniture was enormously heavy, and when we wanted the pool table in the game room moved a bit it took six grown men to accomplish the task. Dining tables were similarly heavy and enormously strong. Most were many, many years old but were almost completely free from mars and dents. This spoke well of the quality of clientele that visited here as well as the durability of the furnishings themselves.

The parlor was furnished beautifully with hand-carved furniture, softly upholstered and supplied with extra pillows. The floors were covered with expensive, genuine Persian rugs of local manufacture. Upstairs, on the open veranda, there were couches, chairs, and tables designed to promote relaxation, where an occasional cool breeze decreased the normal heat of the day. The area was never particularly hot when we visited in mid-June. It was spring-time balmy and very comfortable during this season. The locals told us the lakes had a calming effect on both humidity and temperature, so the place was generally very livable.

Houseboats on Lake Dal (Bill Behrns' collection)

Alongside of the houseboat, a sizeable cook-boat was moored where any kind of food from any culture or nationality could be prepared in totally clean conditions. This boat was busy night and day to see to our needs, and the cuisine was beyond our expectation each and every day. Up to then, I had never eaten better anywhere.

Dinner was an elaborate exercise in propriety and protocol. We appeared promptly at seven p.m., dressed in a clean uniform. Civilians wore slacks, a coat, and tie. It was not quite formal, but it was most certainly proper. Each of us was seated at the ornate, hand-carved table before our carefully prepared place settings and the first of seven courses was set before us. This would be a light appetizer, salad or soup, or perhaps both, to set our palates for the main course. Then bread would be served with fresh butter. The main course was made to our order, whatever type of meal we desired. I most vividly remember their rack of lamb with mint jelly and curried rice. Beverages were diverse and delicate from wines to after-dinner drinks with ice cream or sherbet to follow. Tea and iced coffee were particular favorites and, since Arnie Thompson and I were not drinkers, we stayed pretty much with that. Desserts were cakes, pies, and puddings—you name it they had it, tastefully and artistically presented. Dinner in this place was a beautiful experience lasting a full two hours.

Evenings were spent on the upper deck lounging, relaxing, chatting, enjoying each other's company, and planning the next day's adventure, which would likely include a journey by water to one of the interesting shrines or gardens that dotted the region. Such outings would take most of a day, and the sightseeing was varied and wonderful. I carried a camera and took many pictures, some of which I still have today.

Shikaras sail on Lake Dal (Bill Behrns' collection)

Transportation around the lake was accomplished by means of slender taxi boats called Shikaras that handled all of the traffic across the lake to the city and back, as well as to the various shrines, gardens, and other lovely spots that adorn the countryside near Srinagar. The boats were heavily and richly cushioned and were most comfortable to travel in.

As a passenger in a Shikara, I could look down into the clear waters of Lake Dal and see the bottom, 20 to 30 feet down, as if looking through clear glass. The water was warm to the touch, and it was quite pleasant to dangle fingers in the water as we moved along. If this place wasn't paradise, it was a pretty good imitation.

Lake Dal is the last of a chain of three lakes tied together by narrow waterways that flow downward like stairs from one to another. On these lakes, farmers grow floating farms from one to three acres in size that they tie together by running rope around the girth of the "island" to keep the plants together. The plants are a type of flower used to make flour for pastries and other foods, and the crops are very valuable.

A farmer will monitor his crop until he determines that his plants have used up all of the oxygen and nutrients in the immediate area, and then he will tether one or two Shikaras together, and he and several others will start paddling with small heart-shaped paddles toward a new location.

At first nothing moves, as if the floating plot was anchored to the bottom which it actually never touches, but soon inertia is broken, and by hand paddling, the family or group moves their floating garden to a new position in the lake where the plants can get that which they need, and the process begins again. Seldom are the farms moved more than three hundred feet, but it takes a great effort to achieve this.

Harvesting is done by hand, as is nearly every kind of task done in this locality. Eventually, the Shikara will be piled so high with flowers that it nearly sinks under the load, and then the farmer will paddle to shore to unload his crop for processing. Then he returns for another load, and on and on, until the job is finished many loads later. There is no hurry about this. The rhythm of work is steady but never rushed. It is smooth, constant, unending, and unchanging. It is the rhythm of the ages that lives in this place and among these people. Time and time again, I would see it in the customs of their culture, in the way they lived their daily lives. To this day, I admire who they were and who they still are, for even today, things in the "city of wealth" have changed little since 1944.

The most fascinating thing I saw in Srinagar was the factory where the ornate, complex, and incredibly beautiful Persian Rugs that adorned the floors on our houseboat were made. Arnie Thompson and I toured the facility and were left wide-eyed by what we saw there.

The process of making a carpet was slow, painstaking, and almost unbelievably detailed with each pure silk thread hand installed as part of the tapestry pattern. One thread was passed over the tightly woven hemp backing precisely as the picture it was a part of dictated. This was done with a needle, and when the thread came together on the back side where it began, it was carefully tied in an individual knot by children from six to twelve years old with fingers small enough to tie each individual knot in its proper place, twelve hundred or more knots to the square inch. The children were carefully trained for this job and remained there, working twelve hours a day until their hands grew too large to allow them to complete the intricate task. Then they were excused from this labor and sent off to learn a new manual skill or to fit themselves into part of the agricultural economy. Girls were allowed to work in the factory until they had their first period, and then they were sent off to largely domestic pursuits. This labor practice was ancient and honorable and had been in place for hundreds of years. The product of this child labor is the finest carpet in the world, famous for durability and beauty. These carpets are sold worldwide and are understandably quite expensive, being made of the finest Indian silk in the most vivid of colors and being assembled with such precision and care. Nowhere else have I encountered such careful and labor-intensive manufacture.

In Kashmir, time is of little concern. The quality of the final product is the only thing that matters. I eventually acquired one of those carpets for my present home. There is so much to remember right there at my feet. Today that carpet hangs on my wall as a fine piece of art I wish to preserve as I do my memories of that fine, faraway place where there always seems to be peace and beauty.

I revisited the locale about 40 years later, accompanied by my wife and sister, and found things very much as I had left them during my wartime visiting. Some things and places we hope are eternal. Srinagar is one of my hopes.

Chapter Thirty-Six: On to Calcutta and the Taj Mahal

We remained in Srinagar ten days and then moved on to Calcutta where we stayed another ten, residing once again at the Grand Hotel in the very lap of luxury. There I was reunited with Paula, and Arnie Thompson looked up his local girlfriend to make us a foursome. We spent several days relaxing and unwinding in splendid company, enjoying the fact that we weren't doing a whole lot for the first time in several months. When you live continually with stress, a person tends to discount the constant overall effect it has on the way your mind and body function. It took Arnie and me a full two weeks to return to something approaching normal. It was most pleasant not to have to shake out my boots each morning looking for cobras, not to mention all of the other routine combat zone things we had gotten used to doing. Civilization definitely had its rewards.

Just before we were due to return to Chittagong, Arnie and I decided to make a sort of pilgrimage to see one of the true wonders of the modern world, the Taj Mahal. It is said that any trip to India that does not include a visit to this most spectacular monument is a journey wasted, and after seeing this magnificent building, I tend to concur.

Just getting to Agra, the city where the building is located, was an adventure in itself that illustrated much about the meaning and style of life in what today is called a "third world country." There are three ways to get to the site if you are a tourist. One can fly into a modern airport, travel by road (usually in a crowded bus), or you can take a train. Of the choices available, the train was by far the slowest and most interesting.

Arnie and I caught the train from Calcutta and made a many-hours ride west and north to Agra. Riding a train in India is an experience worth relating since it is so very different from the same kind of trip taken almost anywhere else in the world. Trains were brought to the Indian subcontinent by the British nearly a hundred years ago, and the common people have developed ingenious ways to take advantage of this predictable, reliable way of getting around. You almost have to see the people ride to believe it can be happening.

First of all, trains in India are not very fast by Western standards. They do well to manage twenty-five miles per hour. They also stop frequently, and the result is long hours spent going anywhere that is beyond local. Trains are small, usually no more that five or six cars including a tender behind the engine. The cars are designed to hold about sixty passengers each, but it is not uncommon to find one holding upwards of two hundred people in every size, shape, and condition. Sitting room extends beyond the seats to windowsills and floors so that there is no square inch inside the car that is free from human habitation. We were literally crammed into our seats next to people carrying chickens and goats in their laps or others who carried birdcages with them or packages of market goods. Added to that were the people who were hanging onto the windows from the outside standing on a wooden molding nailed to the bottom of the car. These folks paid no fees for their train ride, climbing onto and off of the train as fancy hit them. I was later told that many of these people have nowhere in particular to go but were actually just along for the ride since it is something to do and therefore better than the nothing they have to do otherwise. Such riders drop off anywhere the train slows down and are liable to jump onto the next train going back, returning to square one after several hours of literally going nowhere. Those of us inside were jammed in like sardines and, with nothing like air conditioning, we were enormously uncomfortable for the entire trip.

As if this wasn't enough already, the roof of each car was similarly jammed with free riders carrying all manner of cargo with them bound for who knows where. Two hundred inside, another hundred outside, and still there were places where people found they could snatch a free ride. The hitches between cars sometimes held three or four hitchers, the tender car had another bunch sitting on the wood used as fuel, the cowcatcher on the front held three more, and so it went 20 miles an hour down the track, screeching horribly from a high-pitched whistle and smelling unbelievably ripe. Fetid air rose from the car windows to be replaced by hot humid air from outdoors, which quickly acquired the inside odors with a touch of sauna. I don't remember how often our train stopped for water and wood, but it was several times, maybe every two hours. At each stopping point, hundreds got on and hundreds got off. New odors were added to old ones, and the process would begin once more.

Several passengers in our car had monkeys with them, which added to the general chaos of the ride. These anthropoid beasts sometimes rode on the owner's lap but most often sat on their shoulder until the animals decided it was time to tour the car, walking on the backs of seats or over various passengers as impulse dictated. In the process they did what monkeys do wherever and whenever they felt so moved, and the odor of monkey dung was added to the mix of things in the car. If you are familiar with this odor you know what I mean since no one ever forgets it. If you are not among the initiated, you really don't want to go there. Odor de monkey is completely beyond description, and everywhere you go in India there are hordes of monkeys, free to come and go as they like, fouling the environment as they do so. They made our train ride a lot less pleasant, as if that could actually have been done. If you've never ridden a train in India, you simply haven't lived. Eventually we arrived at Agra and happily detrained.

We found lodging near the Taj Mahal and spent the night, thoroughly exhausted from having sat in the sardine-can railcar for 16 hours. In the morning, we rode out to the site in a local taxi and hooked up with a tour guide who told us the story of the place.

The Taj Mahal is an elaborate tomb, built by an Indian ruler named Shah Jahan as a memorial to his favorite wife, whose title was Mumtaz-i-Mahal, meaning Pride of the Palace. The name from the building is derived from this title.

The building was under construction for twenty-two years and is made of the finest white marble that could be found. It is the most spectacular example of Islamic art and architecture in existence, although it should be said that some Persian and Indian influences are visible in the structure as well. This wonderful edifice has drawn hundreds of thousands of tourists each year since it was finished in the early 1650s. This monument to unmatched and undying love has stood the tests of time, of the elements, of wars, of political upheaval, and also of religious strife. It is beyond all of those seemingly petty things in its utter magnificence. Mankind has accepted the gift of the husband to the memory of his wife in the spirit in which it was offered. Some minor thefts have occurred over the years involving the rubies and emeralds, which were used for emphasis. All within reach have vanished. Otherwise the monument is little changed since it was completed.

The approach to the monument passes through a carefully manicured park that is cared for entirely by hand. The extensive lawn area was being mowed as Arnie Thompson and I followed our guide up the esplanade past the four minaret towers located beside the hundred-yards-long reflecting pool that dominates the approach.

The man who designed the park area through which we passed understood how to enhance the grandeur of his building by using the repeated image on the water's surface to double the visual effect experienced by the visitors. The building seemed to be both before us and beside us as we walked toward it, all of the time watching a horde of gardeners pushing specially made hand mowers around carefully clipped tree bowls and walkways. Not a single weed could be seen in the thousands of square feet of lawn the men tended. Everything was letter-perfect all day every day.

The Taj Mahal as seen from the Agra approach
(Bill Behrns' collection)

As we moved forward and the building before us became larger in our view, the effect of the pool image became more pronounced. The 133-feet-tall minarets punctuated our journey and added a further dimension to the experience when call to Muslim prayers issued forth from them five times a day. We would be onsite long enough to hear three of those chantings during our visit.

Shah Jahan is buried in a vault next to his wife under the tall dome. Their place of rest is separated from the public area by a tall, semi-transparent screen beyond which the white marble caskets can be viewed. I'm told the proper term for such a container is "sarcophagus," a Greek word that means, "flesh eater." The definition of the term seems appropriate to its task. Like the rest of this incredible monument, the caskets are hand carved from white marble, carefully and intricately engraved by master craftsmen. Their workmanship is better than anything I had encountered before and equal to or better than anything I have encountered since in my rather extensive travels over the following sixty-seven years.

The acoustics beneath the dome are so perfect that a whisper can be heard on the opposite side of the room. Only the Mormon Tabernacle in Salt Lake City is able to compare in quality of sound transmission. The fact that the dome of the Taj Mahal is open to the outside air makes the acoustic perfection even more remarkable.

Each of the huge marble building blocks used in the walls is placed squarely and perfectly upon its mate with no mortar to attach it. No block ever moves for want of glue since each is hand finished to less than a one-thousandth-inch tolerance. At no point in this building is there a place where a single slip of paper can be inserted into a stone joint. The dome is similar in construction with the weight of each stone holding in place those around it through precision of fit. No building anywhere has ever been more carefully made.

The Taj Mahal reflects the lighting at each time of day having a golden cast in the morning sunrise. At noon it takes on a more yellow tone, and at evening it turns pinkish in the sunset. At night the building seems to softly glow blue as if there were some bluish light source within the building. Fine marble is semi-transparent, and the quality of light must first penetrate the surface before being reflected back out. The medium gives the light a soft, almost warm effect, as if the building was somehow alive. The Taj Mahal is said to be the Seventh Wonder of the Modern World, and for this visitor it lives up to that name.

Yes, if you are wondering, there are monkeys at the Taj Mahal. They were of a different species than those we encountered on the train or in Calcutta, being far larger and longer-limbed than their urban cousins. These monkeys were nearer to the size of a Golden Retriever, probably weighing between sixty and seventy-five pounds. They were rangy in build and seemed more comfortable on the ground than they did in the trees, and they had the complete run of the place. There are monkeys everywhere in India, and as was the case elsewhere they had considerably more freedom than most people. If the Hindus are correct in their belief that one returns to life in another form after passing on, a person could do worse than return as a monkey in India.

Our R and R time was winding down, and after an excruciating return trip to Calcutta aboard another Indian train, Arnie and I made ready to return to the war.

The places we had visited had been normal, peaceful places, and it was hard to imagine that a brutal conflict awaited us only a short plane ride away.

Chapter Thirty-Seven: Back to the War

The monsoon season finally abated at the end of September, and those of us enjoying rest and relaxation found ourselves headed back into the war zone. Arnie and I went out to Dum Dum Airport and reacquired our Lightnings for the 200-mile flight over the Bay of Bengal back to Chittagong. We found nothing of concern going on until we checked in and discovered that our last mission had been "scored," and I was suddenly short one shoot down. Al Kocher met me at the flight line as I climbed out of the *San Joaquin Siren* and told me my last kill had been credited to Burdette Goodrich in spite of the fact that he never claimed one for that day, and no one seemed to have reported watching him shoot down anything before he was lost himself. Apparently someone other than I had heard his radio call confirming my kill, and decided it was actually me confirming him. The fact that I had claimed that kill myself was ignored completely. "I'm not taking that flag off our plane, Lieutenant," Al told me, "and I don't care what they say about it!" I agreed with him, and the flag stayed on.

In retrospect, it is amazing how much confusion was engendered by that two-word radio message. I assumed that Goodrich would confirm my kill, and immediately on landing told Al Kocher to paint another flag on my plane, which he did. I then reported my win to my commander, including Goodrich's confirmation. He told me that Goodrich had not returned from the mission. Then we found out that Captain Duke had gone back looking for his wingman, Lieutenant Baumeister, or possibly Goodrich, if you credit Bill Aycock's diary entry, and he had not returned. Baumeister, Duke's wingman, had become separated from the Captain, and Duke was apparently worried about him, or maybe he was worried about Lieutenant Goodrich, although that seems less likely since Goodrich was not part of Duke's flight, and his absence might well have not been noticed by the Captain. In his radio call, Baumeister said he saw Goodrich go down, and someone said that he had gotten himself out of his plane safely, at which point Baumeister radioed that information and Duke reportedly replied, "Okay, I'm going home," after which Captain Duke was not seen again. Baumeister made it home okay. My radio brought me none of this, and I returned to base somewhat oblivious.

Somewhere in the midst of all that, Goodrich's radio confirmation of my kill was heard by someone other than me or was related behind closed doors by Major Luehring, and someone decided I was confirming for Goodrich and that my claim was somehow bogus. All of this went on in a matter of about an hour, and it took sixty-five years to straighten it out. Without help from the Japanese Archives, we never would have gotten it right.

This brings me to a point where I feel obligated to discuss the scoring method employed by the ranking officers of the 459th Squadron and the effect it had on the rank-and-file pilots who served there. After each mission, the ranking "group" gathered in the squadron ready room and decided what had happened and who was to be given credit for what. The official 459th Fighter Squadron history written by Colonel James M. Fielder indicated that pilots were interrogated after each mission, but this was not the case for me or most of my on-the-line colleagues. I can attest that I was never sought out and asked about anything I had done in the air. On a couple of occasions, I went to Major Leuhring and reported things such as my shoot-down over Meiktila, but neither he nor anyone else from the "group" ever sought me out looking for information. Others of my friends on the flight line reported similar experiences, saying things like "they never asked me about that," on several occasions that I remember. I recently spoke by phone with Vic Veroda and asked him for his memories of the after-mission routine, specifically if he was asked for details by anyone at the end of a sortie. "I don't remember anything like that," he told me. "After Major Boggs assumed command, we were given a single shot of whiskey after a mission, but that was the only contact I recall." Any questioning that may have gone on seems to have been confined to that "group of leaders" at their ready room conferences. Line pilots were not interrogated.

Those in leadership roles were Major Leuhring (our commander), Captain Boggs, Captain Broadfoot, Major Glenn (operations officer), Major Webb (executive officer), and sometimes Captain Duke, who was a consistent flight leader. Others in the room, but likely less influential, were Bill Aycock, Lockheed Technical Representative, and Staff Sergeant George Garwood, who served as semi-official secretary, taking notes on the proceedings, a copy of which I possess. Also often present was Captain James Fielder, supply officer and eventual squadron historian. Late in his service Lieutenant Burdette Goodrich began to assume some administrative duties as assistant operations officer and was therefore admitted to the gatherings. It is possible that this closer association with the people who decided things led to Goodrich being given credit for my fifth victory. Goodrich was already an ace, and when I was finally able to prove my claim to that victory it did nothing to diminish him for which

I am grateful since he was a very good friend and someone whom I greatly missed. We hung out together a lot and went on R and R together. I think of Burdette Goodrich often.

During that mission of June 6, there were three aerial victory claims made by Twin Dragon pilots. Only one of those actually happened, according to Japanese Army Archives, and that one was not credited to the pilot who actually scored the victory. It was actually credited to two different pilots neither of whom was actually involved.

Obviously our scoring system was less than perfect. Due to the lack of broad-based investigation of each mission, a lot of valuable information could have been and probably was missed. Major Glenn would eventually claim that he shot down Captain Sumino, but the War Department never accepted that claim, although he was given credit for an Oscar on June 6. The Japanese reported the loss of only one airplane that day. Later on, research in Japan, undertaken on my behalf, proved that plane was flown by Captain Sumino, and that I was the pilot who brought him down. My description of the combat and its result was exactly what the Japanese had reported in their records, so that there could be no doubt of my claim. It took a very long time to find that out, and I will discuss the process more fully later in this text.

In fairness to those involved, I never encountered any negative feelings directed towards me by any of the leaders. It is possible that I might have gained greater access to the group and been perhaps more involved in the decision-making process if I had pushed harder for recognition, but at that time in my life, I was not a particularly forward person, and I did not put myself out front.

The social structure of the unit might also have been an influence. I was not a social drinker like most of the lead group tended to be. I was raised in a home where alcohol was not present, and while I had no aversion to it, I did not indulge out of habit. The leaders could often be found at the bar in the officer's club while my crowd and I would be seated otherwise enjoying Coca-Cola or some other soft beverage, my favorite being iced coffee. The lead group was always friendly towards us but were never really our friends. They had their group, and we had ours. Of all the pilots I knew, only William Orr encountered visible animosity. I will discuss that a bit later.

Within that framework, one needs to add that Captain Walt Duke was friendly toward us all. He was an affable fellow with a well-developed sense of humor who had friends at all levels. We all enjoyed Captain Duke. I don't think he had any agenda other than killing the enemy, at which he excelled. His loss was a blow to the entire squadron. He was the best of us, and we all missed him.

Captain Walt Duke (Bill Behrns' collection)

I can't say that there was ever an attempt by the leaders to deprive anyone of victories earned, although I thought that sometimes they were a little too tight with their interpretations. Twice I shot down planes and watched them disappear straight down into the jungle without being able to add them to my score, since neither of them visibly burned or left an impression on the landscape large enough to be able to locate later. "If you can take me back there and show me the wreck," Major Luehring told me, "then the kill is yours. Otherwise it is just a probable."

Confirmation of victories has always been something of a hit-or-miss process based on often-uncertain information gathered in the midst of a full-out, fur ball dogfight. During such actions, a combat pilot has two principal jobs that take nearly all of his energy: finding and eliminating the enemy and keeping his own hide (and airplane) free of enemy bullet holes. With our heads constantly on a swivel and looking everywhere at once, it was often impossible to find time to assist a teammate by observing a shoot-down all the way to the ground. More than once, a squadron member had reported seeing me "on a target and scoring hits" without being able to follow the action to a kill-confirming conclusion. You did the best you could with the snatches of sight and chance viewings you encountered while watching for Japs, who almost always outnumbered our Dragons. A good, hard look was difficult to come by.

Wing cameras were helpful with targets directly in front of your plane, but they failed to show targets on the numerous deflection shots that sometimes scored deadly hits. The cameras in such cases showed only empty air. There were many ways to wind up with a probable rather than a victory. Proper crediting of air-to-air kills was no easy task for anyone involved.

While I could be mistaken about this, it has always seemed to me that those pilots inside the orderly room were more likely to have their claims confirmed than those of us on the outside. Since I was never privy to those conversations and/or "interrogations" that took place within the orderly room confines, I cannot really say for sure if it brought advantage or disadvantage to any of us. It has been said that "eighty-five percent of success is just showing up," and being inside rather than outside may have been an advantage. Then again, it may not have been.

Still, I wonder if I had pressed my claims harder or somehow found a way into that group, becoming a recognized ace might have happened more quickly than it did. At that stage of my life, I was not the tough, old survivor I became later on, and I allowed things to rest as they were for many years afterward. Eventually it became important to me to set the record straight as I saw it, and I took such actions as I found available in order to achieve what I felt was due. It turned out to be a lengthy process, but well worth the effort.

In Major Leuhring's defense, it must be said that he only allowed himself three aerial victories. Still, those three were enough to gain for him a Silver Star, our nation's second highest award for heroism in combat. Also, rank came very quickly to those inside the group compared to the rest of us, a condition which I believe was common throughout the Pacific Service. Those in command were more easily noticed than were down-the-line pilots or ground crewmen. Headquarters groups also tended to move forward rapidly. There is the right way, the wrong way, and the Army way. Such is the nature of the beast.

Chapter Thirty-Eight: A Bombing Mission, October 13, 1944

On October 13, we were assigned a bombing mission to Mawdauk in support of ground troops who were having a hard time subduing the nearly 25,000 Japanese troops known to be in that area. We were given a bunker position as our main target and outfitted with two, one-thousand-pound bombs apiece with which to suppress that installation. I was given the lead position in my four-plane group with another four planes following. I was flying number 848 this day, giving the *San Joaquin Siren* a day off.

I decided to approach our objective by leading my flight slightly to the south of the target in hope of making us look like we were after something else, thus cutting down on the time available to the numerous Jap antiaircraft gunners we knew were waiting for us. We increased our speed on approach to about 360 miles per hour and dropped down to 14,000 feet to set up our run.

When the city passed beneath my left wing, I turned my plane on her side, did a wingover and pushed down into a 60-degree dive with throttles to War Emergency Power. I was gaining speed very quickly as I approached my release point of approximately 8,000 feet. I was traveling at better than 550 miles per hour by this time, and things were rushing up at me in a hurry, which unfortunately included some antiaircraft screaming up from below. I must have been diving right down that gunner's barrel because my fighter took a hit that instantly shut down nearly everything electric in the plane. I was suddenly plunging down toward the earth with very little control over the process.

My immediate thought was to get free from my payload so I used the manual override handles to jettison the two thousand-pounders still attached to my plane. The bombs came loose quite properly, but momentum being what it was, they continued along the same path as my plane separating them from me by only a scant few feet. For all practical purposes, I still had the evil things. Now I had to get away by creating some space between the rapidly approaching two big bangs and me. Happily, the Lightning's avionics were manual and not dependent on electricity, so I was still able to control the path of my flight as long as I had momentum to carry me. At that moment, I had lots of momentum.

I eased the half-dead plane away from the plunging bombs, and when I reached four hundred (or so) feet, I pulled up hard and brought my Lightning out of her dive and pointed her off toward friendly territory out near the Burma Road. It would be several miles before I would be in semi-safe territory, so I concentrated on making a good glide and getting as far from our target area as I could manage without engines. It was a hectic ride while it lasted, but there was one comforting thing that I specifically remember, which was that my squadron-mates flew through their bomb runs and promptly formed up on my wings to escort me as far as my ride would go. I flew flat and straight, no gimmicks or tricks, until I began to lose speed and altitude. I was preparing myself mentally for a low-altitude bailout that would require me to jettison the canopy, unfasten my belts, and roll the Lightning over, which would drop me out of the plane. At that point, I looked ahead and saw a gray streak against the jungle green. I was looking at the Burma Road. I suddenly knew where I was going and what I would do when I got there. I had sufficient altitude and speed to carry me to that mostly-flat strip which wound its way through the jungle toward the eventual "hump" that separated Burma from China and another part of the war. I believed I could find a place to put my ride down as gently as I could and hopefully get out in one piece. If there was such a place, the Burma Road was it.

There was very little glide time left to me as I straightened out my plane and flattened my approach, hoping not to bounce or spin when I bellied her in. Contact commenced, and I felt the banging and grinding of irregular surfaces beneath the pilot gondola, but the plane stayed down on the softly-ground dirt on the road's surface. Centuries of oxcarts had ground the soil to a fine powder, which was settled during the monsoon seasons only to be reground by the next year's traffic. I was down in something akin to a sand trap and might have skidded smoothly except that my left-hand prop dug beneath the surface and grabbed a deep rut, bending the prop and putting a sudden jolt into the ride. That bit of plowing brought my ride to a sudden conclusion. I deplaned in a hurry and scuttled across the road into the jungle where no marauding Japanese soldier was likely to see me. My escape was partially concealed by an enormous cloud of fine dust thrown up by the dirt-cushioned belly landing of my 12,000-pound aircraft.

I found myself alone in an unforgiving place. Much as I hated to admit it, I had just been shot down.

Chapter Thirty-Nine: A Night in the Jungle

Having escaped from the crash in one piece, I set about finding a place to hide far enough into the jungle to avoid being seen but still close enough to the Burma Road to observe any comings or goings that might occur in the next few hours. Up above, my squadron mates were flying wide circles, dropping down to strafe the roadside across from me to suppress any interest by anyone who might want to come after me. After a few passes, the fighters formed up and headed back to base, leaving me to my own devices until some kind of rescue could be mounted to get me home. It was late in the afternoon, so there was insufficient time to get back from Chittagong before nightfall, so the jungle was going to be my hotel for the evening.

I considered moving farther back into the forest and decided against it. There could be too many unfriendlies back there including king cobras, boa constrictors, pythons, water buffaloes, and Bengal tigers—to name a few. I figured it was better to remain close to the road where things could be more easily seen from selected cover.

I found a large tree with a diameter of about four feet that was enough cover so that I could remain out of sight from the road by staying up against the trunk and moving carefully around it to break up any line of vision. I thought about arranging a bed of some sort and perhaps lying down but abandoned that idea when preliminary scratching with my boots turned up hordes of crawlies from ants to centipedes. I would spend the night on my feet. Tarzan I was not.

I had a few supplies with me designed to get me through

such situations, and these gave me some comfort as I prepared to settle in for the night. I had my Army issue .45 pistol and a military combat knife for weapons. Also there was a survival kit containing mosquito repellant, water purification tablets, pills for malaria, a syringe of morphine, a signaling mirror, some bandages, and some chocolate bars. I was neither helpless nor likely to starve. Still, I was edgy and nervous as darkness descended on a Burmese jungle that now contained a kid from French Camp.

Hours passed slowly, and I moved about around my tree listening to strange sounds coming from the bushes behind me. Some of those sounds were probably monkeys, numerous in the area and very active at night. Other small animals would pass nearby, making sounds in the twigs and vegetation, keeping me alert. As midnight approached, I began to think I might make it through the night without a major incident, and then all of that changed when the jungle went unaccountably quiet. Something else had entered the equation, and my animal neighbors were aware of it. I soon began to realize I was in the proximity of a powerful foe. A Bengal tiger had come upon my hideout and seemed to be trying to locate exactly where I was. I never saw him, and thankfully he never laid eyes on me.

Every now and then, the cat would cough, hoping the sound would cause movement he could hear or see, revealing the hiding place of that which he sought for prey. I had heard that sound before while deer hunting at night at Chittagong. It was a hunting technique as old as time, and I did not fall for it, though I must admit my nerves were stretched pretty thin. I kept still and quiet, moving ever so slightly and quietly around my tree, keeping the trunk between my deadly companion and myself.

After a while, the tiger would cough again and listen. Each time this happened over the next few minutes, I adjusted my cover as quietly as I could and hoped I would not have to go one-on-one with the acknowledged King of the Jungle. In close night combat, the great cat had all of the advantages, and while a man with a .45 could kill such a beast, it would be difficult to get off an accurate shot before the cat could employ the arsenal of weapons he carried with him. I carefully continued my tree dancing until finally the predator lost interest and left the area as quietly as he had come. How long we danced together I really can't say, but the jungle slowly became noisy again, and I was very glad to hear it. The rest of my night was uneventful. The unknown can be very frightening, but the known is sometimes more so.

Vic Veroda told a story about waking up one night while sleeping in a basha at Chittagong and finding himself staring face-to-face at a full-grown Bengal, just inches away. Across the narrow isle Vic's roommate, Tony Greco, was making small squeaking noises trying to get Vic's attention without stirring up the feline visitor. "He was a big brute," Vic said, "but he made no noise at all."

The cat looked Vic over carefully and then turned and walked back outside as quietly as he had entered. In the morning, large pugmarks were found between the beds in the basha proving the visit was not a dream. We knew about tigers. We lived with them.

Sunrise was a blessed relief. I now had a reasonable command of my surroundings since I could once again see them, and I felt certain my Dragons would soon arrive to take me home. I did not look for pugmarks but moved my hiding place closer to the road where I expected to soon see action. This proved to be true.

Salvation appeared in the form of a Douglas A-24 Dauntless dive-bomber flown by my friend and confidant Arnold Thompson. Along as escorts were four P-38s who circled about as top cover while Thompson put the Dauntless down. I aided the process by moving out of the bush onto the road and using my signaling mirror to attract attention. The planes spotted me almost as soon as I appeared, and they set up for the snatch-and-run maneuver they had planned back at base.

Lt. Arnie Thompson in his usual P-38J. Arnie was one of my closest friends in the squadron, along with Burdette Goodrich. (Bill Behrns' collection)

The Dauntless had wide wings and very large flaps to accommodate landings on aircraft carriers, and it was ideal for a landing on the Burma Road. Furthermore, the Dauntless was a two-man plane, and there was room for me to climb aboard in the rear seat, which I very quickly did. Once I got settled in the back seat, Arnie gunned the Dauntless and we took off, joining our escorts for a pleasant run back to Chittagong and safety.

Over the years, I have had occasion to wonder what the squadron would have done to rescue me if we hadn't stolen that A-24 from Dum Dum Airport in Calcutta a few months before. Dum Dum was a huge facility, and there were literally hundreds of airplanes sitting along the runways unattended. Every so often, one of them would vanish into thin air to show up on some other base as an extra for guys like Arnie and me to work out in. We had the A-24 for quite a while at Chittagong before it turned out to be a lifesaver on the Burma Road. We acquired an AT-6 Texan the same way from the same place on a different "midnight requisition" run, and it also made its way into our history. Don't believe everything people tell you. Sometimes crime does pay!

When we landed at Chittagong, Major Luehring and our flight surgeon, Doctor Simmons, met us at the flight line and asked me if I had suffered any injuries. I replied that I was fine, "Fit as a fiddle," I said, and was immediately returned to active duty.

"Do you see that P-38 right over there?" Major Luehring asked me.

"Yes, sir, I do," I replied.

"Well, that is your plane for today's mission. Get ready, we're going out in a few minutes."

Old West psychology says that when you get bucked off your horse get right back on." My commander had just given me today's horse, and I got aboard and flew off for another run at Japs.

The mission turned out to be a milk run, but it was a good thing to do. I had no time to feel sorry for myself or develop some sort of a complex over having been shot down. I was back in the air, back on the ground and having an iced coffee just a day after riding a dead fighter plane to the ground and spending a long night in the jungle. No harm. No foul.

The next three missions were routine, which brought us to October 22, which was anything but ordinary.

Chapter Forty: The Siren Becomes Air Corps History

On October 21, 1944, First Lieutenant John Burger was assigned to fly to Tegzon from Chittagong to pick up some supplies. John was one of my close friends within our squadron, and when he came to me and asked to borrow my plane for the flight, I agreed to the arrangement. Burger went out to the flight line and put the *San Joaquin Siren* in the air for what should have been a very ordinary flight. The *Siren* carried two, three-hundred-gallon belly tanks with her, modified to carry the cargo John was expected to deliver back to Chittagong at the end of his trip. Little did any of us know where this simple-sounding sortie was going to lead us.

Burger flew the *Siren* over to Tegzon, our former base, once called Kurmitola, and spent the night before his planned return the next morning. The events following were unexpected and sadly memorable. Much of what I am now reporting comes from a restricted War Department Army Air Corps report since I was not there to see what transpired, and I am frankly glad that I wasn't a witness.

Burger's takeoff on the morning of October 22 drew little attention but that changed rapidly. John apparently climbed to an altitude of around 8,000 feet and then did a wingover and came down Devil-for-Leather to buzz the base. People on the ground could hear the pitch of the *Siren*'s engines change to a loud, uncomfortable scream as she roared over the buildings about three hundred feet above the ground, wide open at more than four hundred miles per hour. All ground personnel were alert by now and heading outside to see what kind of banshee was assaulting their position. They soon found out as Burger climbed back to altitude and lined up for another pass. The second time down was faster than the first and also at a lower altitude.

One report had the *Siren* at maybe 12 feet above the ground when he began to collide with some trees. Another report said that a flight of birds, perhaps crows, rose up in front of the plane just as it neared the trees and became involved with the aircraft causing the pilot to abruptly lose altitude (of which he had precious little) and dip his wing, which caught the trees changing his pitch suddenly. This contact caused the P-38 to cartwheel into the ground twisting and tumbling for more than five hundred yards, taking out three buildings including the 89th enlisted men's mess hall and an outhouse, before coming completely apart.

As the plane disintegrated, parts and pieces of buildings flew on ahead toward an embankment just across Roosevelt Road, on which two enlisted men were then walking. One of the men, Sergeant Paul Bradshaw, saw the wreckage coming at him like a Pacific tsunami and attempted to pull his companion, Sergeant Peter Olenik, down into a ditch for cover. Sergeant Olenik apparently misunderstood because he pulled away and remained standing while Bradshaw dove down and away to safety. When the wood and metal storm passed by, Bradshaw emerged from cover to find half of Sergeant Olenik lying across the road.

Wreckage from the *Siren* was scattered over 1,500 feet, with the engines being the last things to stop moving. Of the pilot, Lieutenant John Burger, very little was recovered. The official forensics report listed part of one foot including most of the ankle and a section of lower spine. Rumors among our pilots mentioned part of a skull and a ribcage, but since these items did not find their way into the official report, I tend to discount their discovery. When all was said and done, there were three men killed, eleven injured, and three buildings completely destroyed. Most important in this tragedy were the loss of an experienced combat pilot and the P-38 he was flying, my *San Joaquin Siren*. I grieved for her quietly for quite some time. The *Siren* had been a fine war partner, and she had gained for me many honors as we flew the Burma skies together. I was never attached to another airplane as I had been to her. Not even the wonderful P-38-L5-LO I was given as her replacement could capture my heart and mind as the *Siren* had done. Even today, I think about her with warmth and affection. Some things shared in the heat of battle cannot be properly communicated beyond those who survived them together. We made war on our enemies together. We evaded attacks, dodged bullets, survived being hit, and returned home on one engine together. I scored my fifth victory and qualified as an ace while flying the *San Joaquin Siren*. Her influence upon my life has been profound. There is so much I remember about her. Our Muslim friends have a saying that fits here. "Speak their name and they live again." The *San Joaquin Siren* lives within me.

My crew chief, Al Kocher, shares the *Siren* experience with me, although on a somewhat different level. Al said many times "I have my plane, and I have my pilot."

He meant that then and as one of the few survivors from that time and place, he still means it today. I spoke with Al several times by phone during preparation of this book, enlisting from him things only he knows. Al has been very helpful with the details of maintenance. The plane may be gone, but Al Kocher still has his pilot. Another participant in the *Siren* experience was Lockheed Technical Representative Wayne Sneddon, who was daily involved in keeping our planes flying. He had his pilots and his planes. Without the tireless and effective labor of these men, we pilots could not have effectively contested against the Japanese, let alone defeated them. I owe those guys, and I will not forget them.

Post Mortem

The Air Corps launched a thorough investigation of Tegzon mishap, which they labeled "The Crash of the San Joaquin Siren." Several documents from that probe served as sources for this chapter. As a result of their findings, a confidential bulletin was issued to squadron commanders in the Pacific Theater urging them to tell their pilots not to buzz bases. Along with the bulletin, a poster was sent that was put up on bulletin boards throughout the Theater showing pictures of the damage resulting from the *Siren*'s bloody end. The poster read, in part, "This damage was not the result of an attack." "Don't work for the enemy!" The poster was 24 x 30 and featured photos of the ruined buildings as well as a total-cost figure for the crash: $150,630.00 according to the Air Corps, something in excess of $350,000.00 dollars if the cost of the P-38 is included.

That poster got around. I have spoken with several other Pacific Theater pilots who remember seeing it at their bases. The *San Joaquin Siren* had become something of a household name in our part of the war. I still have a copy of that poster.

*Bill holding Air Corps poster on San Joaquin Siren crash
(Ken Moore photo)*

Chapter Forty-One: A New Assignment: The 58th F/S-33rd FG

On November 5, 1944, I was transferred out of the 459th to the newly formed 58th Fighter Squadron, 33rd Fighter Group that was being put together at Sahmaw Field in Assam, inland from the Bay of Bengal and three hundred or more miles from Chittagong. Major James Ward was in command of the new group, and he requested four pilots, including me, from the 459th to serve as instructors for new pilots he would be getting in shortly. The 459th was being moved south, looking for more enemy action. When the 459th left, there would need to be a unit in the area to assist the retaking of Burma by Allied ground forces. That unit would be the 58th FS.

When I arrived at the new base, we had no airplanes and no pilots, although we began getting new aviators very quickly. At Shamaw, we were short of large permanent buildings so the pilots and crewmen lived in a tent city not far from the small operations building. As he had when we first met, Major Ward instructed me to put my things in his tent, which I did. We had

Major James Ward (Bill Behrns' collection)

gotten on well the first time we met, and we would do so again now.

Planes followed a few weeks later, and transition training began as wings became available. Some of our pilots were experienced, and others were definitely fresh from the box. One of our new guys was just 18 years old. None of them had ever flown a Lightning before. We jumped headfirst into the training program and soon had P-38s in the air.

It was December 22 before I flew my first mission from Sahmaw. It was a four-plane patrol mission, and I was leading it. On December 30, I led another four-plane mission to bomb infantry positions. These were routine assignments because we saw no Japanese aircraft and encountered sporadic ground fire for opposition. As things turned out, we never again encountered the 64th Sentai that had been our adversary since our arrival in CBI. The word we got was that the 64th had been moved north, much closer to the home islands, to counter the growing Allied naval advance that was headed their way. From here on in, there was much less risk to us as we carried out our sorties.

We flew a lot of missions out of Sahmaw, flying every two or three days as weather permitted. We seldom encountered heavy action so our Lightnings were rarely in need of patching up.

We flew quite a number of "patrol" missions that were moderately relaxed opportunity flights where we went out and looked for trouble. We seldom found much to do in the air since the Nips had withdrawn their air cover, but we were able to gather aerial intelligence on the numbers and disposition of enemy forces. Several times, I flew these missions in an AT-6 trainer that carried no guns or bombs. The Texan, as she was called, was very agile and could fly lower and slower than our P-38s and was therefore ideal to someone to use as an eyeball platform. I could spot things from the AT-6 that a pilot in a higher and faster Lightning might very well miss. Also the Texan was an excellent aerobatics plane, and in the right hands could avoid enemy fire quite readily. The AT-6 also allowed me to watch the younger pilots perform in case instruction was needed. I liked that little plane a lot and enjoyed flying it. The fact that I felt no need of armament said a lot about the kind of missions we were flying at that time.

When new planes began to arrive, there were several P-38L-5-LOs among them, and I was assigned one of those new, state-of-the-art fighters. The L had more horsepower than any previous Lightning. The L also had dive-flaps and hydraulic-assisted steering that helped it to react more quickly than previous models and also turn tighter since maximum lock could be achieved and maintained more easily. The dive-flaps solved the compressibility problems by pushing the turbulent air coming off the wing surfaces back past the horizontal stabilizer, giving the plane clean air in which to fly. This advance allowed us to take full advantage of our Lightning's incredible diving speeds. The L model also had more fuel capacity and a different intercooler set up than previous P-38s. There was a "Christmas Tree" rocket set up near the tip of each wing, which added to our firepower. It was a great flyer, very likely the best plane in American service at that time.

As the new assignment moved onward, we continued flying close-air support for ground troops, usually well in advance of American units moving up on the retreating Japanese. My memories of this period and the missions it contained are not nearly as sharp and clear as many I have from the 459th. This is no doubt a function of the fact that no notes were taken in post-flight meetings that I have been made aware of. There is nothing in print beyond mission assignments, and no one has brought forward a 58th FS diary that would give my memory the boost it needs after sixty-five years of passing time. Also important was the routine nature of flying missions against minimal opposition. No one lost and no one injured was the summary of most of the assignments undertaken by the 58th during the five months I flew with that group.

My situation was very different with the 58th than it had been with the 459th. In the 58th, I was flight leader on nearly every mission I flew, while I had been wingman for most of my 459th flights. Toward the end of my stay with that original unit, I began to find myself in tandem with Captain Duke, and after we lost him, I began to be cast as element-lead, usually with Major Webb or Major Glenn as flight leader. At the very end of that deployment, I began leading missions myself. Once I arrived at the 58th, I was immediately put in the lead position. This transition proved to be easy enough, and I had no problems with the added responsibility, and I must say I was proud to be out front.

We began getting new pilots for the 58th before we had planes for them to fly, and since these men were combat veterans from other units for the most part, there was little ground school needed beyond reading the P-38 flight manual, which they could do on their own. Once we began to receive new Lightnings, there began an intensive transition program to make the new guys twin-engine capable and comfortable with their new mounts. Each 459th veteran took charge of a student and began to familiarize him with the more complex systems they would be using and getting him in the air as fast as possible. After a couple of weeks, we had enough planes and pilots ready to be able to plan and undertake missions against enemy targets, and Major Ward began sending out flights of four or eight planes for bombing and strafing runs on infantry-support targets. I did not yet have a plane of my own, so I was at loose ends for a few days.

To fill in the idle time, I set out to learn the flight characteristics of a British leftover we inherited when we took over the Sawmah Base from them. They left a perfectly fine and fully fueled and loaded Republic P-47D Thunderbolt sitting alongside the runway with no one in charge of it. As one might expect, the kid from French Camp took charge of the orphan and set about learning to fly it. The results would prove to be interesting.

Chapter Forty-Two: Flying the P-47

Having spent several hours in the AT-6 Texan while waiting for my new combat ride, I became intrigued by the possibility of learning a new plane. The P-47D was just sitting there day after day, with no one to care for or about it, and I decided after a while that I should have a go at it just for fun if nothing else. A search of the squadron office produced an operations manual for the big Republic fighter, and I settled down for a few hours of reading before tackling the airplane head on.

Nicknamed the "Jug" by the pilots who flew her, the P-47 was also known as the "Farmingdale Fatty" for her outsized fuselage and the town in New York State in which she was built. The P-47 featured a Pratt and Whitney "Double Wasp" 18-cylinder radial engine that produced just above 2500 horsepower. Big as she was, once off the ground the Thunderbolt was a capable fighter, although nowhere near a Zero for maneuverability. The big plus for the Jug was her ability to absorb punishment and keep on flying, something the Zero simply could not do. The premier Japanese fighter owed its agility to lack of weight achieved by eliminating armor for the pilot and puncture sealant for the fuel tanks. A Nip pilot could turn and move with the best, but if hit by Allied tracers, his plane was likely to explode, catch fire, or

Republic P47 Thunderbolt

simply fall apart. A Zero pilot was not well protected while a P-47 pilot was.

Robert S. Johnson, one of America's leading aces in Europe, told a story of running out of ammo in his P-47 and having to endure a thorough working-over by an Me-109 that he could neither fight nor outfly. The German sat behind him and seesawed back and forth across the stern of Johnson's Jug until he finally exhausted his ammunition. Failing to knock his enemy down, the Kraut drew up alongside, saluted Johnson and flew off for home, leaving the American to live another day, if he could somehow fly safely back to England in a plane that was plainly shot all to hell.

To Johnson's surprise, the big Jug flew just fine in spite of resembling Swiss cheese. When he landed in England, Johnson's crew chief counted over one hundred holes in the back of the plane. Somehow no control lines were severed. No doubt about it, Jugs were tough.

The big disadvantage that came with the Thunderbolt was its rather limited range of 450 miles. This meant that anything over 200 miles from home base was out of range. Even with 160-gallon drop tanks, the thirsty Double Wasp engine limited the range dramatically. Our Lightnings were capable of over 3,000 miles without refueling so there wasn't much comparison. Still both U.S. and British forces flew a large number of Jugs during the war, although they were of more use in Europe than they were in our theater.

There it sat on the edge of the runway as if looking for company, and I went out to see if I could provide aid and comfort. I was amazed by the size of the beast. The P-47 was over 14 feet tall at the tip of the cowling, and her 40-foot-plus wingspan added to the overall feeling of size. I climbed into the cockpit and found myself in a suite rather than the office

I was accustomed to in my P-38, and being a small guy to begin with, I felt slightly overwhelmed. The large pilot seat, referred to by some as a "lounge chair," was comfortable, and from there I could reach everything, so I soon felt more at home. The instrument panel was intelligently arranged. The cockpit was "air conditioned," which in that day meant it was heated.

I took the next hour getting used to the location of key instruments and finding necessary switches before I attempted to fire the plane up. To my surprise, she took hold on the first half dozen revs and ran smoothly and powerfully right from the get-go in spite of having been sitting for at least three weeks unattended.

I advanced the throttle a bit and began to taxi the aircraft, getting the feel of the controls and judging her response to them. I didn't much like the tail dragger confirmation, but having spent many hours in the AT-6 Texan recently, I was accustomed to it and had no problems as I snaked my way from side to side down the runway so that I could see ahead over the massive front cowling.

Control response was good through the conventional flight stick. An index finger trigger for the guns was located at the top front of the stick as it was in most other American fighter planes. The airplane went where I wanted it to go without any need to adjust things. She seemed to be in good overall order, so I decided to go for the gold and put her in the air.

I taxied to the end of the strip, turned into the wind, called the tower for permission, and when that came I pushed the throttle forward and headed off for the wild blue assuming this oversized bird would take off like everything else I had flown. The Thunderbolt left the ground easily and climbed nicely to one thousand feet. I tried a few easy moves and found her responsive and very controllable. As it turned out, the fat lady was a good dancer, and I became immediately very comfortable with her.

As I came back by the field, I saw a group of P-38s taking off for a mission, led by Major Ward. I swung in behind the eight-plane flight and moved up even with the lead, just as Major Ward called me on the radio. "Bill, how's your fuel?" he asked me.

"It's full, sir," I replied.

"You got ammo?" he came back.

"I'll check," I replied. I eased over a bit to clear a safe field of fire, activated my gun switch and pressed the trigger. A sudden roar of eight, 50-caliber machine guns answered my command. "Yes, sir. Loaded and hot," I said happily.

"Come on along," the Major said.

"Glad to, sir," I answered and fell in behind the eight-plane formation in a tail-end-Charlie position. I was on a mission in a P-47.

It was a short flight to target, just over one hundred miles, and when we arrived the Lightnings made a run at a supply depot next to a railroad yard, dropping their thousand-pound bombs as they hurried past. Having no bombs aboard, I remained at altitude and flew top cover until the attacking Lightnings re-formed for a strafing run. This I was well equipped for, so I found a place in line and followed a Lightning down for a gun-pass. My plane did a good job, giving me a line and visibility along with copious firepower. I found a building to shoot at and shredded the roof wonderfully before pulling back up into formation. It was a good, clean pass, and I liked the feel of it.

On the way back to base, we looked for targets of opportunity but found nothing of interest. The new guys were elated, of course, and did aerobatics and sang songs on way home the way the Twin Dragons had done in the early days. "I've been working on the railroad, all the live-long day. I've been working on the railroad just to pass the time away..." The time passed, and we came home unhurt.

As I approached the field, I suddenly realized that I was in for another adventure as the words of Mr. Caradies from Hancock Academy echoed in my mind. "Behrns," he had said. "There are two things you have to learn to do. You have to get the plane off the ground and then get it back on the ground. All of the rest comes later." I had just skipped the second part of that first all-important lesson. I had never attempted to land a P-47. So here I was, once again a rookie.

I decided to bring the Jug in a little bit hot, landing at 105 miles per hour rather than the 80 to 90 called for in the training manual. The one thing I didn't want to do was stall. The next thing I hoped to avoid was the beginner's bounce I had managed so wonderfully between two lines of B-24s at that secret base back in Arizona. So I came in fast and flat, and the big Republic fighter touched down as softly as a falling Aspen leaf. The Jug had proven itself to be very controllable, and I had enjoyed my day in it.

I checked with some pilots and found that I had burned nearly twice the fuel of most of the P-38s flying with me. There would be some missions where the Jug would have to remain home for lack of the long legs necessary in CBI.

The day had been something of a lark, a bit of fun, something different, but truth be known, I was more than pleased when a couple of days later, Major Ward presented me with a brand new P-38L-5-LO and told me I would be leading missions in that plane as soon as I could check her out. I was more than happy to be back in a Lightning.

Chapter Forty-Three: Over the River Kwai

Several of our 58th FS missions as well as previous sorties with the 459th were designed to slow or stop supplies moving to Japanese Army units traveling on the South Burma Railroad, known as the "railway of death," which became famous when a French novelist named Pierre Boulle wrote about his experiences as a POW forced to work on construction of that line. He titled his book *The Bridge Over the River Kwai*, which was widely read after its publication in 1952. The railroad and its forced labor construction crews became very famous when David McLean made the story into an Academy Award winning movie in 1957, staring Sir Alec Guinness, William Holden, Jack Hawkins, and several other notable actors.

The now-famous bridge talked about in the movie never crossed the Kwai River at any point, actually being built across the nearby Mae Klong River, renamed the Khwae Yai (Big Kwai) in the 1960s in order to accommodate the large number of tourists who came looking for the place where McLean's movie happened. This misinformation seems to have been a mistake on the part of the author rather than intentional misdirection which was used to a large extent throughout the novel that depicted a British POW group under command of a Colonel Nicholson who decided to assist the Japanese with the building of their bridge in return for better treatment for the men under his command.

The actual officers the author had in mind were French rather than British, and the British commander involved did not collaborate with the Japs in any way, shape, or form.

Lieutenant Colonel Phillip Toosey, in command at the British end of the line, resisted the Japs every way he could and still remain alive. People who survived those camps have said that no British officer would have lived long if he had collaborated. His own men would have "quietly eliminated" him. The French, on the other hand, were different. They not only collaborated in the Pacific but also in Europe and North Africa. The Vichy government was the worst of those representing a country normally on the Allied side.

During the nearly two years it took to build the railway that ran past Rangoon all the way to Thailand, 13,000 POWs died, and more than 100,000 civilian conscripts also perished; many of them were buried along the route. Conditions in the camps were in reality much worse than those shown in the movie. The enormity of Japanese brutality is difficult to adequately describe without an "R" rating and a stronger stomach than I have. If you want a more detailed look at it, James Clavelle provides it in his novel *King Rat*. While this excellent novel does not examine collaboration, it does show the reader the inside workings of a Japanese POW camp in the Singapore area from a mostly British viewpoint.

While flying missions for the 459th and later the 58th, none of us ever saw a big, stout, well-constructed bridge we could use for a target. We did provide top cover for B-24 Liberators and B-25 Mitchells, who did that work at altitudes considerably lower than where our Lightnings were during these escort missions. On occasions, we carried one-thousand-pound bombs that we used to destroy approach ways to those river crossings.

We flew from this time on in support of Allied armies commanded by General Stillwell, Colonel Merrill (Merrill's Marauders), General Wingate, and others. Our patrols gave us an opportunity to knock out bridges, trains, and suspected supply depots. If an Allied army ran into heavy interference, we were called in to bomb and strafe the enemy. This would soften them up and enable our armies to proceed.

One day with the 459th, our planes shot up an infantry unit marching up the approach to a bridge. According to intelligence we received later, we killed 18 of them and wounded a bunch more. Harassing missions like these took up most of my remaining days in CBI. Our aerial combat was over. My last combat flight was April 14, 1945.

We also flew a lot of "patrol" missions that looked for targets but seldom found much. Enemy power was moving out of our area. The war in Burma had morphed into an infantry grind against a steadily retreating Japanese Army no longer intent upon annexing India. The Empire was shrinking all throughout the Pacific Theater. The British, under Lord Mountbatten, were getting stronger, and our American naval power, both surface and air, was pushing northward toward MacArthur's return to the Philippines and the eventual struggle for control of the Japanese home islands. In this setting, American airpower transformed itself into close air support missions in which small arms fire and dwindling antiaircraft were our chief obstacles. Like we had with everything else sent our way since we arrived in CBI, we went right after it. Twice I had one engine shot out and returned to base on a single engine. Several other times my plane took hits, but none was critical.

Incidentally, we never did make it into the movies.

Chapter Forty-Four: Going Home

Although I argued against it, my friend and tent mate, Major Ward, insisted on making a night flight to Madras, India, to see a movie actress he had known in the States. She was there entertaining the troops. He made it to the base but unfortunately crashed into a tree and was killed on landing. A new commanding officer was then sent to join us. After a couple of months, he decided the 110-degree, 100-percent-humidity weather was no deterrent, and since this was a military base, henceforth we would all wear shirts and ties. I said, "Not me." Since I had gone several months over my normal rotation time, I decided to return home.

On the last night while preparing to leave for the States the next morning, two of our pilots went out and shot two little barking deer. They returned to camp and hung them up in a large oak tree in the middle of our compound for the butcher to prepare in the morning. During the night, a member of our group went outside his tent and in the moonlight saw a huge tiger standing beneath the tree preparing to jump up and get the deer. He picked up his 30-caliber rifle and shot the tiger. When I came out in the morning, I went over and picked up its head for a picture. The picture has since been misplaced, but the memory of that last night on base still remains.

My trip home took me first to Calcutta, across India to Karachi, and then next to Cairo, Egypt. I stayed in Cairo for five days at the Shepheard's Hotel and became friends with an American aircraft carrier pilot staying there. We toured the Sphinx, the Pyramids, and old town Cairo. From there, I flew to London and then on to Washington D.C. After a stay of two days in Chicago, I headed to Los Angeles, where I caught a bus to Bakersfield and then a train to Stockton.

After two years and three months, I was once again home. I had thirty days leave, so on the second day I took our ranch truck and started hauling livestock. The money was very good, so I separated from the service and stayed in trucking for 12 years. I married and had five children: four girls and a boy. As trucking profits fell off, I sold out and opened a store with my best friend. Then after twenty-three years of marriage, my wife and I realized we lacked love and decided to divorce; however, we have remained good friends ever since.

The next change in my life was when I sold out to my partner and decided to get a real estate and insurance license. I then became a land salesman with Boise Cascade. I now had an airplane and enjoyed five years with Boise Cascade as a manager. After those five years, most of the good land was sold, so I moved on to the insurance business, becoming a manager with a major company. I worked there for six years before opening my own agency. I remained self-employed until my retirement at age sixty-seven.

In 1975 I married Cheryl Kathleen, and we have enjoyed thirty-six years of the happiest, most loving time of our lives. With God's help and direction, we will remain that way for the rest of our lives.

On Veteran's Day, 2000, my wife Cheryl put my picture in the Stockton Record, our local newspaper. Immediately Cecil Kramer called, introduced himself, and invited me to a meeting in Sacramento with a P-38 group called the Fork Tail Devils. Cecil is a noted P-38 historian with abundant knowledge of his subject. Since then, Cecil and I have given more than 60 speeches. We have participated in many air shows as well over the years, and we are still at it today.

In 2004, Greg Zola called from Chicago and said he wanted to build a model of the *San Joaquin Siren*. After three years of research and several thousand dollars, an exact replica of the *Siren* was completed. It was absolutely fantastic with a nearly ten-foot wingspan, counter-rotating props, and even a small pilot. Greg brought the model to Stockton, and we took it to a model airport. A large crowd was on hand to witness the P-38 in flight. It was a beautiful sight, but unfortunately, upon landing in a heavy crosswind, a wing dipped, and the plane was damaged. Greg has the parts, so in the future the *San Joaquin Siren* will take to the sky once again.

The one goal that still remained for me was to get credit for the fifth kill that my good friend, Burdette Goodrich, received instead. As stated earlier in this book, on June 6, 1944, Goodrich stated that he would verify my kill, but he was then shot down and soon died taking that verification with him. Without verification or a proper investigation sixty-six years later, I still did not have credit for the kill, but things finally began to change when I heard from Colonel Tolliver from San Diego. He heard that I was trying to prove that I had shot down the plane in question. He contacted Yasuho Izawa, a medical doctor and a PhD, who had access to Japanese records from the war. His detailed history of the Japanese Air Force included information about Goichi Sumino who was shot down on June 6, 1944. The account parallels exactly what I had reported. With this information I received help from Congressman Pombo and after he was out of office, Congressman McNerney came to my aid. The Air Force still insisted that the kill would have to be verified. However, Congressman McNerney presented me with the U.S. Defense Medal for serving in Olympia Washington, which was declared a danger zone, and I also received my third Distinguished Flying Cross at that time.

The state did not follow the same rules and regulations as the Air Force. In 2008, Alan Nakishi from the California State Assembly took up my cause. He presented the facts to the assembly body, which included a letter from the archives including a picture, and they voted on it. This became resolution #1944. He then called me to the capital and presented me with the resolution. In the audience was Bob Miller, an official with the American Aces Association.

The following morning at our meeting in Sacramento of the Fork Tail Devils, Bob announced my acceptance into the rank of aces. So in 2008, I became a World War II American Ace. This would never have happened had not Cecil Kramer brought up my case to Alan Nakanishi.

My Life in a Nutshell

Text and Music by Bill Behrns 2011
Transcription by James MacQueen

2

Biography of William (Bill) M. Behrns

Bill Behrns began life, in 1920, as a three-month premature baby, weighing barely three pounds. He grew slowly, but size had no bearing on his ability to play ball and outrun the other kids. By the age of six, he was driving a team of mules and soon after, one of their farm tractors. He received his driver's license at the age of 14.

After high school, Bill spent three years in college. Prior to completing his degree, he landed a lucrative sales position with Standard Oil. After 15 months, he transferred to management in a federal government job at Benecia Arsenal.

During this time, Bill's buddies took him to an air show to watch America's two premier pilots, Roscoe Turner and Tex Rankin. The excitement consumed him and he decided then he would become a pilot and fly P-38s.

Bill was drafted in December of 1941. Through ingenuity and risk-taking, Bill seized an opportunity to take the Air Corps flight exam and passed. He excelled in flight school and in June 1943, graduated as a commissioned officer and P-38 pilot. He had realized his dream.

Eventually, Bill was sent to active-duty in the CBI (China,

Burma, India) Theater of War, as a member of the 459th Fighter Squadron. Behrns flew 104 combat missions with the 459th. He shot down five Japanese Fighters in the air and destroyed six on the ground. After 13 months with the 459th, Bill was invited to be a part of a newly formed squadron, the 58th Fighter Squadron 33rd Fighter Group. Bill transfered as a transitional training officer for new pilots. Because the Japanese had withdrawn all of their planes but left their armies, the squadron's mission was then to soften up enemy armies and enable allied armies to overcome their threat. Behrns' last mission was April 14, 1945. After a month of leave, he was sent on a new assignment to fly P-80 Shooting Stars.

Bill left the service in August, 1945, to establish a livestock trucking company. After 13 years of decent pay but small interest on his investment, he sold his company in favor of joining a partner in a retail store. After 12 years, he sold his interest in the store and joined Boise Cascade as a manager in land development and sales. Six years later, he chose a new opportunity in management with Bankers Life Insurance Co., and after five years, he developed his own company. He retired at age sixty-seven.

Bill Behrns holds the American Defense Medal, the C.B.I. Combat Medal, and the Distinguished Flying Cross with two oak leaf clusters. He also holds the Air Medal with two oak leaf clusters, the Unit Presidential Citation, and the Good Conduct Medal.

In later years, he has given more than 60 lectures to schools, businesses, and airports. He has also been invited to participate in air shows from Pennsylvania to Oshkosh and points beyond. In good health at the age of 91, Bill Behrns is still on the move.

Biography of Kenneth S. Moore

Author Kenneth S. Moore, was born and raised in Santa Maria, California. All members of his family were involved in education. His father was a principal and superintendent, and his mother and sister were both elementary school teachers. So, of course, Ken became a teacher as well. After graduating from Sacramento State with a master's degree in history, he taught a variety of subjects at the junior high school level for twenty-five years, but he enjoyed teaching history the most.

Ken was a man of many interests including racing Porsches and excelling in golf. After retiring from teaching in 2001, he continued working with young people as a founder and coach with the Stockton Junior Scholastic Trap Association. Hunting waterfowl, deer, and game took him to Mexico, Argentina, and Africa.

Ken was an avid reader, amassing a wealth of knowledge about the Civil War and World War II. His interest in combat aircraft and World War II led him to two groups in

Sacramento, California, where former pilots from World War II met monthly. It was at these meetings that he met Bill Behrns, a P-38 pilot and World War II ace. After several years of gentle coaxing, he talked Bill into letting him write about Bill's experiences, which became this book, *The San Joaquin Siren*.

The San Joaquin Siren was almost completed when Ken passed away unexpectedly in May of 2011. Ken's wife of 40 years, Tina, graciously and proudly brought together and finished the book for him. The night before Ken passed away, he received notice from Amethyst Moon Publishing that they would be honored to publish the book. Writing a book and completing it was Ken's lifelong dream.

CPSIA information can be obtained at www.ICGtesting.com
Printed in the USA
BVOW020500311011

274885BV00004B/6/P